Odysseus Elytis

Odysseus Elytis, 1978

Odysseus Elytis

Analogies of Light

Edited by Ivar Ivask

University of Oklahoma Press : Norman

By Ivar Ivask

Luminous Reality: The Poetry of Jorge Guillén (coed.) (Norman, 1969)
The Cardinal Points of Borges (coed.) (Norman, 1971)
The Perpetual Present: The Poetry and Prose of Octavio Paz (ed.) (Norman, 1973)
World Literature Since 1945 (coed.) (New York, 1973)
The Final Island: The Fiction of Julio Cortázar (coed.) (Norman, 1978)
Eluƙogu: Selected Poems 1958–1978 (Lund, 1978)
Odysseus Elytis: Analogies of Light (ed.) (Norman, 1981)

Library of Congress Cataloging in Publication Data
Main entry under title:
Odysseus Elytis: analogies of light.
    First published in the autumn 1975 issue of the quarterly, Books abroad.
    Bibliography: p.
    1. Elytes, Odysséas, pseud.—Criticism and interpretation. I. Ivask, Ivar, 1927–
II. Books abroad.
PA5610.E43Z82   889'.132   80–5240

Contents

Illustrations

The vignettes in this book are by Odysseus Elytis, done for the "Book of Signs," a small volume of aphoristic sayings published in 1977. All have been slightly reduced from their original size.

"Votive Offering" (1973), Collage by Odysseus Elytis

Preface

It is not exactly the rule that small literatures, however long and illustrious their past, are recognized with two Nobel Prizes in successive decades. Neither is a critic often vindicated through a Nobel Prize a few years after he has ventured to proclaim a poet one of the three greatest produced in the twentieth century in his language. Yet this happened in the case of the 1979 Nobel Laureate, the Greek poet Odysseus Elytis, who was selected sixteen years after another Greek poet, George Seferis, received the same literary accolade in 1963. The Autumn 1975 issue of *Books Abroad*, still the most comprehensive critical presentation of Elytis in a major Western language, was singled out by the Swedish Academy in its bio-bibliographical notice on the laureate and the critic-editor graciously invited to witness the award presentation ceremonies in Stockholm. In a way the Elytis issue of *Books Abroad* helped make literary history. Therefore we are happy to bring this tribute to the Greek Nobel Prize Laureate back into print in book form. The discussion of Elytis's poetry has been updated with an interpretation of his recently published major poem *Maria Neféli* (1978) by M. Byron Raizis. The photographic record, the chronology and bibliography have also been made current.

In his Nobel Lecture, Elytis chose to speak "in the name of luminosity and transparency." It is hard to imagine better terms than these to introduce the fundamental creative preoccupations of a lifetime. These qualities are revealed in his poems and essays, collages and translations. In a world of murky ambiguities Elytis's Mediterranean faith in light and its analogies is truly *salutary* (which etymologically means "promoting health"). The work of this modern Greek poet embodies elements which our gloomy, pessimistic, cynical age desperately needs: a charge of light and vitality instead of one more recapitulation of the poisons and shadows which surround and penetrate us. Elytis's poetry opens up light-filled, oxygen-rich vistas, as does the Greek archipelago or an ascent to Mount Parnassus. This is not to say that his mythic vision is not edged by a profound awareness of the forces of tragedy and evil, chaos and war in which he himself participated as a lieutenant in the Albanian Campaign of 1940–41. However, darkness and chaos do not prevail. His poetry constitutes one more memorable gift of Greece eternal to the world. His "Silver Gift Poem" expresses beautifully the essence of this generosity. I quote it in the translation by George P. Savidis and Bette Anne Farmer (from Elytis's collection "The Light Tree and the Fourteenth Beauty," 1971):

> I know that all this is nothing   and that the tongue I
> speak has no alphabet
>
> Since both the sun and the waves are a syllabic script you
> decipher only in times of sorrow and exile
>
> And our land   a mural with successive overlays Frankish or
> Slavic   and if you try to restore it you are immediately
> arrested and made answerable

To a host of foreign Authorities   through your own always

As happens in disasters

Yet   let us imagine that on a threshing-floor of olden times
which may well be in a tenement house   there are children
playing   and that the loser

Must according to the rules   tell and give the others a
truth

So that in the end they all find themselves holding in their
hand a small

Silver gift poem.

IVAR IVASK

Norman, Oklahoma

Odysseus Elytis

Analogies of Light:
The Greek Poet Odysseus Elytis

By IVAR IVASK

> *The lesson remains the same: it is sufficient to express that which we love, and this alone, with the fewest means at our disposal, yet in the most direct manner, that of poetry.*
>
> O. Elytis

The endeavor to follow several contemporary literatures does not result in an increasingly unwieldy aggregate of names, but rather the very opposite: the more literatures one studies the shorter is the list of essential authors who can withstand the test of constant comparison. Exposure to literary quantity can sharpen one's sense of enduring quality. There is no need to exalt a second-rate poet just because he happens to write in your native language, when you are aware of a first-rate poet in another literature who does the same thing so much better. Misguided patriotism due to linguistic parochialism vitiates more than one overblown literary reputation. The Lithuanian poet Henrikas Radauskas once formulated what appears to be a veritable law of literary physics: "The smaller the country, the fatter the anthology." (And, one might add somewhat facetiously, the more geniuses per square mile.) Yet there *are* exceptionally creative marginal literatures and insufficiently translated major poets in minor languages! What is therefore more needed than ever is the continuous critical exploration of the entire contemporary literary spectrum, which would entail challenge and recognition of universally valid achievement wherever realized.

There is no denying, for example, the scope and depth of the Greek literary renaissance in our century, particularly in the field of poetry. Constantine A. Trypanis claims with authority in the Introduction to his pioneering bilingual *Penguin Book of Greek Verse* (1971, p. lxv): "Poetry written in Greek constitutes the longest uninterrupted tradition in the Western world. From Homer to the present day not a single generation of Greeks has lived without expressing its joys and sorrows in verse, and frequently in verse of outstanding originality and beauty. . . . It is a happy augury that in the last hundred years better poetry has been written in Greek than in all the fourteen preceding centuries; and that in the last fifty years . . . Greek poetry has again achieved universal validity and significance." Although Trypanis's selection spans close to three millennia from Homer to Odysseus Elýtis, it is understandable that those last fifty years can hardly be exhaustively presented in such a vast context. The English-speaking reader is fortunate to be able to supplement it with Kimon Friar's massive *Modern Greek Poetry: From Caváfis to Elýtis* (New York, Simon and Schuster, 1973), which presents thirty poets on 780 pages; there is also Edmund

Keeley and Philip Sherrard's earlier *Six Poets of Modern Greece* (New York, Knopf, 1961), which offers a more limited selection. The latter two translators have reduced their choice even further in their *Four Greek Poets* (Harmondsworth, Penguin, 1966), which includes Caváfis, Seféris, Elýtis and Gátsos.

Not wanting to miss for a moment the complete modern Greek poetic landscape as traced by Friar, I personally feel most convinced, from a comparative perspective, of the major status of three outstanding peaks: Constantine Caváfis (or Cavafy), George Seféris and Odysseus Elýtis.* The English-speaking reader who wants to become acquainted with these three Greek poets is again in a uniquely favored position, since almost their entire poetic production is available in reliable translations, often in exemplary bilingual editions. Cavafis (1863–1933), the poet from Alexandria, is even accessible in three collected editions: John Mavrogordato's *The Poems of C. P. Cavafy* (London, Hogarth, 1951), Rae Dalven's *The Complete Poems of Cavafy* (New York, Harcourt, Brace & World, 1961) and Keeley and Sherrard's new translation—the most complete and easily the best that is available—of the *Collected Poems* (Princeton, N.J., Princeton University Press/Bollingen, 1975). As to Greece's only Nobel Prize winner to date (in 1963), Smyrna-born George Seferis (1900–71), we have Keeley and Sherrard's bilingual volume *Collected Poems 1924–1955* (Princeton, 1967, 1969, 1971) and Walter Kaiser's translation of the later *Three Secret Poems* (Cambridge, Ma., Harvard University Press, 1969). An interested reader can further consult *The King of Asine* (London, Lehman, 1948), versions by Bernard Spencer, Nanos Valaoritis and Lawrence Durrell, and Rex Warner's *Poems* (Boston, Little, Brown, 1960). Rex Warner and Th. D. Frangopoulos have translated selected essays by Seferis under the title *On the Greek Style* (Boston, Little, Brown, 1966), and Athan Anagnostopoulos is responsible for the English version of Seferis's *A Poet's Journal: Days of 1945–1951* (Cambridge, Ma., Harvard University Press/Belknap, 1974). Until 1974, poems by Elytis (b. 1911) were available in English translation only in anthologies and various literary journals. Then in 1974 all this suddenly changed through the almost simultaneous publication of two books (by a strange coincidence, both published in Pennsylvania): Kimon Friar's generous selection of poems from the years 1935–73 entitled *The Sovereign Sun* (Philadelphia, Temple University Press, 1974; for a review see this issue of *BA*, pp. 830–31) and the complete version of Elytis's most important longer poem to date, *The Axion Esti* (Pittsburgh, University of Pittsburgh Press, 1974; see

---

*Saying this, I am fully aware of the growing reputation of a fourth modern classic, Yánnis Rítsos (b. 1909). However, his immense productivity—over forty books to date—has not yet been brought into as sharp a critical focus in one representative collected volume of translations as has the more restrained output of the other three major poets. This certainly is not the fault of Rítsos, but merely one of the limitations which must be accepted by those friends of Greek letters who are dependent on quality translations. Nikos Stangos's translation of *Selected Poems* (Harmondsworth, Penguin, 1974), with Peter Bien's fine Introduction, is a step in the right direction. (See also Peter Bien, "Myth in Modern Greek Letters, with Special Attention to Yánnis Rítsos's *Philoctetes*," in *BA* 48:1, pp. 15–20).

I would also like to note that I have thus far referred to the Greek poets by using the accented forms of their names. The names of Caváfis, Seféris, Elýtis and Rítsos—and also that of Níkos Kazantzákis—are by now sufficiently familiar to the English-speaking reader, however, and will appear without accents throughout the remainder of this issue, except where they are listed otherwise in the title of a book or article.

this issue of *BA*, pp. 829–30), with facing Greek text, translated by Edmund Keeley and George Savidis. Since Elytis is just as accomplished an essayist as was Seferis, a liberal choice from his "Open Book" in English is an urgent need.

It should be evident from the foregoing that the interested reader has available in English the full panorama of Greek poetry in the twentieth century, complete with major and minor figures. Three masters of universal fame, Cavafis, Seferis and Elytis, are accessible in fairly complete editions. Hardly any other literature of a small nation has fared so well in English as has the poetry of the modern Greeks. The present *Books Abroad* number joins in the tribute to a supremely creative minor literature and one of its major figures. (Since our Winter 1969 issue, a special Greek section directed by Kimon Friar has systematically charted the latest developments in this literature.)

*

I met Elytis for the first time around midnight near Syntagma Square on the eve of Greek Independence Day, the first without the Junta, 25 March 1975. All Athens was in flags. My wife and I arrived by bus from Patras for a two-week stay in Greece. It was our second visit. The first was back in the Spring of 1961 when I bought my first copy of *To Áxion Estí* in Eleftheroudakis's bookstore. I bought the book as a symbolic gesture, since I had already discovered and liked Elytis some years earlier. To be exact, this was when I was a fledgling professor at St. Olaf College and had come upon Friar's Elytis translations in *Wake 12* (Winter 1953) and *Accent* (Summer 1954). In March 1968 the poet sent me a few of his books with personal inscriptions, and we exchanged some letters in connection with his first presentation in *Books Abroad* in the Spring of 1971 and his participation on the 1972 jury for the *Books Abroad*/Neustadt International Prize for Literature (see *BA* 46:3, page 428); health reasons prevented his coming to Oklahoma at that time, and he delegated Kay Cicellis to come as his proxy instead. Now Elytis had accompanied Kimon Friar at this late hour to meet us, and not only Kimon, but also the Greek poet seemed like an old personal friend. I had seen Elytis in photographs before, but what struck me immediately was the mixture of gentleness and firmness which marked both his speech and his manner.

We met Elytis soon thereafter for lunch in "Floca," a well-known restaurant on Venizelos Street, and talked for several hours about his poetry, his essays and the translations of his poetry in various languages. He maintained that his essays, gathered in the "Open Book," constituted an essential part of his oeuvre in which the poetic element was fused with autobiographical reflections and objective evaluations-interpretations. Purely scholarly elucidations did not interest him. He was rather skeptical about how soon Greek readers and critics would fully grasp the message of his essays. It would probably take years, he mused, since sophisticated criticism with a cosmopolitan flair was almost nonexistent in Greece.

Our longest visit took place in the poet's small apartment No. 13, Skoufa Street 23, on the evening of 27 March. Elytis pointed out with some pride that he used to be able to see from his small balcony both the Acropolis and the Aegean Sea (and on very clear days even the island of Aegina, where he spends his summers writing), but the view is now obstructed by various new buildings erected in recent years. Still, when standing on tiptoe in front of his bathroom mirror one could see the Acropolis strangely perched atop one of the buildings. Thus, while shaving in the morning he faced the great past of his country, and stepping out onto the balcony, he could perceive the Aegean present, so important to his poetic inspiration. The few rooms of his apartment were simplicity itself: a wall lined with books in the living room, a framed photograph of a dark-haired muse here, a sketch by Tsaroúhis which was not used for a certain book there . . . Before I started taping the interview which follows on the next pages, the poet offered us "Byzantine" coffee (since the term "Turkish" coffee, as Elytis pointed out with a twinkle in his eye, was out), whiskey and pistachio nuts. As a consequence of the latter, our French dialogue on the tape is punctuated by the cracking of pistachio shells (and the occasional wild honking of impatient cars from down Skoufa Street). Was it really a dialogue? It was more a passionate monologue which I was privileged to hear and record. Elytis had much to say. Several statements were made from previously prepared notes. For this reason I eliminated my own interjections and questions, streamlining Elytis's thoughts into a more or less continuous, self-sufficient text. Everything that had to do with the poet's self-interpretation certainly was left intact. What I chose not to include in the present version were, for example, some comments on Mallarmé ("I still like the incantatory quality but not the preciosity of his poetry"), on the growing politicization of poetry today (which he deplored) and on the possible influence of existentialism on his poetry (which he doubted). Listening carefully again and again to the tape when transcribing it, these seemed marginal vignettes, merely random remarks in comparison to what was uppermost in the poet's mind that particular evening in Athens: to communicate his thoughts about his own poetry. This is what Odysseus Elytis wanted to transmit to our number dedicated to his work. For me his poems are in many ways allied to the poetry of such other great European contemporaries as Jorge Guillén in Spain, René Char in France and Boris Pasternak in Russia. These poets have found new sources of individual human dignity and creative freedom without committing themselves to any ideologically restrictive utopian dogma. The experience of their poetry liberates the reader.

1975

Odysseus Elytis on His Poetry

From an Interview with IVAR IVASK, *in Athens, March 1975*

The first thing I would like to tell you is that very often people ask, and in a way they are right, how it is possible to combine in one person, in one poetry, the Mediterranean world—more specifically the Aegean, a motif of my poetry—with surrealism. This seems to be paradoxical, they say. However, it all depends on the perspective from which a thing is seen. For me the Aegean is not merely a part of nature, but rather a kind of signature (as one critic rightly observed). I and my generation—and here I include Seferis—have attempted to find the true face of Greece. This was necessary because until then the true face of Greece was presented as Europeans saw Greece. In order to achieve this task we had to destroy the tradition of rationalism which lay heavily on the Western world. Hence the great appeal of surrealism for us the moment it appeared on the literary scene. Many facets of surrealism I cannot accept, such as its paradoxical side, its championing of automatic writing; but after all, it was the only school of poetry—and, I believe, the last in Europe—which aimed at spiritual health and reacted against the rationalist currents which had filled most Western minds. Since surrealism had destroyed this rationalism like a hurricane, it had cleared the ground in front of us, enabling us to link ourselves physiologically with our soil and to regard Greek reality without the prejudices that have reigned since the Renaissance. The Western world always conceives of Greece in the image created by the Renaissance. But this image is not true. Surrealism, with its anti-rationalistic character, helped us to make a sort of revolution by perceiving the Greek truth. At the same time, surrealism contained a supernatural element, and this enabled us to form a kind of alphabet out of purely Greek elements with which to express ourselves.

This interpretation might help explain why I was so strongly attracted by surrealism, above all by its theoretical side, and how at the same time I adapted it in a Greek way. Some time ago I was visited by a young woman who was writing her doctoral dissertation on French and Greek surrealism. Although she was very young, I realized that she grasped all this very well. She explained that surrealism had proven fruitful in Greece because the Greek surrealists did not simply copy the French, but rather adapted surrealism to Greek reality. This is true. Every one of our so-called surrealist poets has done something altogether different with surrealism: Embirícos, Engonópoulos, Gátsos, Sahtoúris have all done something different, and I have done something else. Obviously, I was never an orthodox surrealist. Nevertheless, I considered surrealism to be the last available oxygen in a dying world, dying, at least, in Europe.

Surrealism also stimulated us through the great importance it placed on the senses. Everything was perceived through the senses. I, too, have brought to poetry a method of apprehending the world through the senses. The ancient Greeks, of course, did the same, except that they did not have the notion of sanctity which only appeared with the arrival of Chrstianity. I have tried to harmonize these two terms; that is, whenever

I speak of the most sensuous matters, I conceive of them as being in a state of purity and sanctity. I aim at the union of these two currents. I am not a Christian in the strict sense of the word, but Christianity's idea of sanctification I do adapt to the world of the senses. This characteristic trait may be indispensable for the better comprehension of my poetry. In my recent collection "The Light Tree," for example, I speak of very abstract things, but always via the senses. The senses do not necessarily possess erotic connotations for me, since they have an aura of sanctity; the senses are elevated to a level that is sacred.

I would like to discuss another matter with you, namely, my Greekness. This is for me not a national or a local thing. I have never been a chauvinist in any way. Greece represents for me certain values and elements which can enrich universal spirits everywhere. Being Greek, I try to present precisely these values on a universal level. It is not a nationalist bent which animates me to do this. To understand all this better, I have developed a theory of analogies. In my volume called "Open Book" there is an essay on Picasso written in French (see this issue of *BA*, pp. 649–51). I speak of analogies there. By "analogy" I mean here that, say, a line a painter draws is not limited to itself alone but has an "analogy" in the world of spiritual values. Seeing the mountains shaped this way or that way must have an effect on the human spirit, must have its analogy. Once you accept this theory, you will be able to see that my fondness of the Greek landscape is not a form of nationalism, but rather an effort at transposition. I have read that a great French architect said the line of mountains near Athens is repeated in the pediment of the Parthenon. That is a perfect analogy!

My theory of analogies may account in part for my having been frequently called a poet of joy or optimism. This is fundamentally wrong. I believe that poetry on a certain level of accomplishment is neither optimistic nor pessimistic. It represents rather a third state of the spirit where opposites cease to exist. There are no more opposites beyond a certain level of elevation. Such poetry is like nature itself, which is neither good nor bad, beautiful nor ugly; it simply *is*. Such poetry is no longer subject to habitual everyday distinctions.

I would now like to say something about the question of language. I believe that the Greek language does not support that attitude toward life which the French call *maudit*. A "poésie maudite" is not accepted by the Greek language. It is difficult to explain this. I try to do so in my "Open Book," yet it is difficult even for Greek readers to decipher this. To put it briefly, I am convinced that every language elicits a certain content. It seems to me that right now we are passing through a period which has a different attitude toward language, an attitude which I consider dangerous. Language is increasingly considered to be no more than a means to transcribe, to express certain convictions, to communicate a state of mind. True poetry, however, is always a creation from within language and not from without it. Ideas are born at the same time as their verbal expression. Hence, the language factor plays an important role. I repeat: I believe that every language makes a poet express definite things. This may seem paradoxical; yet the Greek language does not, for example, accept expressionism—that is, excessive exaltation. It is a lean language which elicits a lean content. This may not suffice for an explanation, but then I would have to recount to you my entire book of essays! To put it somewhat differently, I have reached the conclusion that I am not permitted to vilify life [D. H. Lawrence's phrase "to do dirt on life" comes to mind. —I.I.]. The Greek language insists on a noble attitude toward the phenomenon of life. Of course, it is a personal interpretation I give you here and I may be mistaken, but at least that is the way I see it. Perhaps it is this underlying attitude which has given rise to the claims that I am an "optimistic" poet. Indeed if one excludes the *maudit* attitude as a possibility, then the result may well seem optimistic to some. But believe me, I have never picked up a pencil simply to write that something was like this or like that! I have always been preoccupied with finding the analogies between nature and language in the realm of imagination, a realm to which the surrealists also gave much importance, and rightly so. Everything depends on imagination, that is, on the way a poet sees the same phenomenon as you do, yet *differently* from you.

I would now like to speak about the role of nature. Nature has become something of secondary importance in this age of technology in the West. Nature does not speak to the young today; they consider it as something flat, uninteresting. Yet I think that along whatever path man searches for truth, he is bound to arrive at nature. As I myself once wrote, if nature did not exst, it would have to be invented, because otherwise one could not be. The final goal of every exploration is inescapably nature. This, obviously, is very much part of the Hellenic tradition.

It seems that all I have told you so far has been concerned with the difficulties a foreigner encounters in comprehending my poetry. You would assume that at least the content and the thematics of my poetry, that which we perceive through our senses, would be more accessible. But is it? If I say in Greek, for example, "olive tree" or "sea," these words have completely different connotations for us than, say, for an American. The sea for us is something very familiar and not at all savage; it is like a second earth to be cultivated. You may have noticed that in my poetry I have often referred to the sea as a garden. I do this because the sea is something as familiar as a garden and accompanies us wherever we go.

Another aspect of language poses still another difficulty. As I told you before, I am one of those poets who work from within their language. This is not a detached attitude. I do not think of something and then *translate* it into language. Writing is always an experiment, and often I am guided by language itself into saying certain things which I otherwise might not have thought of. I have been criticized for using certain rare words. But I *want* the text to be completely virginal and far removed from the everyday usage of words. I would go so far as to say I want it to be *contrary* to colloquial usage. The tone of my poetry is always somewhat elevated. I situate the words in such a way as to bring out their rarity. The poetry written after my generation is, as you know, altogether different, since it employs the language of the street and approaches prose. I am not saying that this is better or worse. All I can honestly say is that I don't understand it. This is not my concept of poetry. Why not? Because the poet should strive for *something which is pure.* (I have a longer poem, still unpublished, which is called "Maria Neféli" [Maria Cloud], where I make a concession to this rule. It is a strange kind of poem. In it a girl speaks. Her words are on the left side of the page and the poet's reaction is on the right. Yet it is not a dialogue, but two monologues side by side. It will be my first poem which takes place in an urban environment.) The success of a poem's language depends on the way in which it combines certain words. We do not think of this in everyday speech. We say "Give me a cigarette" or "How are you." Nothing new is said this way. There is no sense of surprise. In a poem, however, one should have the surprise of expression. Your reaction should be: "Look, no one has thought before of juxtaposing these two particular words!" Suddenly, we feel as if an electric current had passed through us. In everyday speech this current is absent.

You ask me whether there is a relation between my concept of elevated language in poetry and my preoccupation with the sacred. Perhaps I have thought of it unconsciously. Actually this is an old tradition in Greece. Just think of Solomós, a great poet who unfortunately is unknown because he is untranslatable. Then there is Kálvos, who has tried for similar effects. In France, there is the lineage of Mallarmé, whose diction is exactly the opposite of colloquial discourse. Even in Éluard we find words we would not have thought of stringing together. In all these cases there is an element of surprise which excites the mind and permits one to see the world from a different angle.

You raised a point in connection with my interpretation of the Greek language as not permitting the *maudit* attitude. How does one, then, account for such poets as Cavafis, frequently considered a Greek *maudit*, and Seferis, characterized by some critics as pessimistic. I would reply that Seferis is not pessimistic but somber. Yes, he is somber, but he never vilifies life. He has that respect toward life which has existed in Greece ever since antiquity. This is also true of Cavafis. He was an unbeliever because he did not believe in anything except sensuality. His language may appear to be colloquial, but actually it is not. It is not easy for a foreigner to detect this, since Cavafis employed a mixture of the purist's *katharévousa* and demotic language. This mixture cannot be transposed into any other language, yet it permitted him to write from a certain verbal distance. There are certainly colloquial expressions in his poetry; after all, it has an urban setting. Nevertheless, there is always in Cavafis a respect for the phenomenon of life as well. Cavafis has a language of his own, a new manner of expression whose great value lies precisely in the fact that no one else before him had thought of writing that way. This I admire. There is, however, another side to Cavafis with which I am not at all in accord. He is very much *en vogue* nowadays. I am not denying that he is a great poet. But I believe that his renown, his glory, will lessen somewhat in the future. I have written that the world of Greek poetry is like a globe whose North Pole is Solomós and whose South Pole is Cavafis. These two poles represent two points of view which between them span an entire world.

I would like to point out another matter. I have never employed ancient myths in the usual manner. No doubt it is advantageous for a Greek poet to employ ancient myths, because he thus becomes more accessible to foreign readers. A Greek poet who speaks of Antigone, Oedipus, et cetera, moves in an area which is well-known; through these mythical figures he can comment on contemporary events. This was done by Sikelianós and, above all, by Seferis. In the case of Seferis it was almost natural, because he was influenced not only by his own Greek heritage but also by the manner of Eliot.

Ritsos, too, especially in his latest period, employs figures from mythology and Greek tragedy. I have reacted against this, often quite consciously, because I thought all this was a bit too facile, yes, even in the theatre. Many French and other European writers have, as you know, adapted the Electra myth, among others. Since my chief interest was to find the *sources* of the neo-Hellenic world, I kept the mechanism of myth-making but not the figures of mythology. Let me explain this. One poem of mine is called "Body of Summer." It is the idea of summer which is personified by the body of a young man. In one of my first poems I have a girl who turns into an orange; in another poem a girl one morning becomes a pomegranate tree. This is the mechanism of personification which I employ here, myth-making, if you wish, but *without* evoking any mythical figures. The Swiss critic Hilty (*Neue Zürcher Zeitung*, 17 July 1960; see this issue of *BA*, pp. 674–78) has rightly observed that in my "Six and One Remorses for the Sky," virtue, which for the Romans was represented by Virtus, is for me a little girl, Arete, who goes everywhere there is evil and beams rays of light into the darkness. Again, this is the mechanism of personifying abstract ideas, yet without turning them into recognizable figures. It may pose difficulties for some readers. You will find this kind of personification chiefly in my first period.

There are three periods in my poetry. I did not consciously arrange my books this way. It is only after having written them that I realize this to be the case. In my first period nature and metamorphoses predominate (stimulated by surrealism, which always believed in the metamorphosis of things). In my second period, including *The Axion Esti*, there is greater historic and moral awareness, yet without the loss of vision of the world which marks my first period. The world has remained for me the same down to the present day. I do try to change my expression, however. I do not want to write continually in the same way, because I have the feeling then of repeating myself. I want to find new forms, new ways of expression.

Let me now make a parenthesis. In one essay in my "Open Book" I tell of the time when I was in Paris, in close contact with René Char and to a lesser degree with Camus. One day I was told that they intended to publish a journal called *Empédocle*, which was to be based on Mediterranean values. These values existed in the work of both of them already, and I was also asked to collaborate. I was to write down in an article the ideas I had developed in our conversations. So I began to write an article which was to be entitled "Toward a Lyricism of Architectural Invention and Solar Metaphysics." The journal soon foundered, and my article was never written. Nevertheless, the idea stayed with me. When I speak of solar metaphysics, I mean the metaphysics of light. Since the sun has always had a central place in my poetry, I called it *solar* metaphysics. All this characterizes the third period of my poetry, my third cycle, if you wish, which is represented by the collection "The Light Tree and the Fourteenth Beauty" (1971). These are simple poems in appearance, but they are difficult to understand. The book appeared only three years ago, and there is no criticism in Greek yet to prove that each poem is a development of the ideas I mentioned above. I have learned to be patient. *The Axion Esti* needed four to five years before it was properly understood. Who knows, perhaps this time it is my fault and not that of my critics. I don't know.

My new long poem "Maria Neféli" belongs to the third period. I've finished the first version, but I'm not satisfied with it yet; I must rework it. It is approximately the same length as *The Axion Esti*, but its structure is even more complex than that of the latter. I am aware that the average reader is not interested in the design underlying a poem. I, however, set up difficulties expressly in order to be able to overcome them, in order to restrain myself, to make myself operate within set limits. It is for this reason that I speak of "architectural invention." I explain this in my "Open Book." One could not imagine, for example, the cathedral of Chartres on Delos. There is always this analogy between nature and language in their eliciting definite forms. Why does a certain church require a certain type of architecture? The same is true of the long poem, where one needs the counterpoint of analogous parts to achieve a certain architectural design.

"Maria Neféli" means "Maria Cloud." Both names have a mythological connotation. But in my poem Maria is a young woman, a modern radical of our age. My poems are usually rooted in my own experience, yet they do not directly transcribe actual events. "Maria Neféli" constitutes an exception. Having finished *The Axion Esti* (this was sixteen years ago), I met this young woman in real life, and I suddenly wanted to write something very different from *The Axion Esti*. Therefore I made this young woman speak in my poem and express her world view, which is that of the young generation of today. I am not against her, for I try to understand her viewpoint and that of her generation. I attempt to understand her by having us speak in parallel monologues. My conclusion in this poem is that we search basically for the same things but along different routes.

You wonder whether "Maria Neféli" constitutes a kind of *summa* of my third period just as *The Axion Esti* stands out from my second period. I don't know. The third period is already finished in my mind. It includes one more unpublished work which I have not titled yet. "Maria Neféli" is the other half of me; it is as if you would see the reverse of me. Already in my early poem "The Concert of Hyacinths" I wrote, "On the other side I am the same." So, here I am showing the other side of myself. Perhaps this poem does constitute the synthesis of my third period.

For the better understanding of certain of my poems, I would like to point out that there are elements which tend to be repeated and to return of their own volition in all three periods. These elements form a sort of framework like that which holds up a building. For example, I have told you that the sanctity of the senses is important to me. There is also the concept that things, when carried to their extreme conclusion, will meet. If you intensify white, you will arrive at black; if you intensify black, you will arrive at white. It is important to keep this concept in mind, because if one does not know it, my later poems may indeed often seem difficult to penetrate. And then there is the development of instantaneity, by which I mean an event which happens in a split second but which can be made to include much more; the instant can be enlarged upon. I have a poem called "Delos" in the collection "The Light Tree." What is this poem all about? It describes a dive into the sea. It is an instantaneous sensation. Yet what you actually feel during the moment of diving is a great variety of things which can later be developed. Or take my book "Six and One Remorses for the Sky." There is a poem in it which begins with a swallow passing before my eyes. This action, which could be contained in a single line, instead grows and forms the rest of the poem. This is what I mean by development of an instantaneous impression.

There is in my poetry a kind of meteorism; there are creatures who have a tendency to mount up into the sky, to rise toward the heights. The Second Lieutenant in the Albanian campaign is dead, but yet he rises; Constandínos Paleológhos falls, but he always rises again. This happens all the time in my poetry.

Let us return once more to my familiarity with the sea. There is a poem—Kimon Friar has translated it—in which I say that the girl who comes from the North is brought by the North Wind. In the same poem, and this seems puzzling, I say, "This sea will revenge itself one day." What is involved here? Well, I consider the sea to be the heir of the Hellenic tradition. The North Wind comes from Constantinople, you understand. But it is the sea which possesses all the values of the Aegean world, and it eventually will take its vengeance. These are some of the things which readers have difficulty in comprehending. It may be strange, but in my poetry the spirit inevitably assumes the shape of a girl, a young woman who has wings and can fly. This occurs repeatedly.

There is a search for paradise in my poetry. When I say "paradise," I do not conceive of it in the Christian sense. It is another world which is incorporated into our own, and it is our fault that we are unable to grasp it. Somewhere I have said that we suffer from a lack of happiness because, through our own fault, we do not know how to grasp it.

Since the sea means so much to me, you ask me whether I know Gaston Bachelard. Of course I know Bachelard; all of his works are on my bookshelf. Which would be my favorite of the four elements? They must be air and water, since these predominate in my poetry. As you well know, there is no denying my islander's side, and so the sea is also present. In another place in my "Open Book" I relate how in my youth I traveled southward for the first time to the island of Santorini, to the center of the Aegean. I had the feeling of being someone who had inherited all these seas as his personal domain. I have had this feeling since my earliest years. When I happened across the theory that Atlantis, a sort of lost paradise, may have been Santorini —which exploded through volcanic action and sank into the center of the Aegean—I could believe it. That's the location of the Atlantis of which Plato speaks as a kind of paradise. Yes, I find even in the depths of the sea the kind of paradise which I seek! Water, consequently, may well be my favorite element. Yet air is significant too, since there is always in my poetry that meteorism, something which irresistibly wants to rise higher.

It has been said that I am a Dionysian poet, particularly in my first poems. I do not think this is correct. I am for clarity. As I wrote in one of my poems, "I have sold myself for clearness." I told you that I am critical of occidental rationalism, skeptical of its classicism, and that I feel the breach opened by surrealism was a real liberation of the senses and the imagination. Could one possibly conceive of a new classicism in the spirit of surrealism? Is this a contradiction in terms? Do you know the work of Hans Arp? There you have great simplicity! He is a classical sculptor, isn't he? Yet he was a surrealist! In other words, the world of surrealism had its classicists *and* romanticists. Essentially, it was a romantic movement. But Éluard, for example, I personally find more classical than romantic.

I never was a disciple of the surrealist school. I found certain congenial elements there, as I have told you, which I adapted to the Greek light. There is another passage in my "Open Book" where I say that Europeans and Westerners always find mystery in obscurity, in the night, while we Greeks find it in light, which is for us an absolute. To illustrate this I give three images. I tell how once, at high noon, I saw a lizard climb upon a stone (it was unafraid since I stood stock-still, ceasing even to breathe) and then, in broad daylight, commence a veritable dance, with a multitude of tiny movements, in honor of light. There and then I deeply sensed the mystery of light. At another time I experienced this mystery while at sea between the islands of Naxos and Paros. Suddenly in the distance I saw dolphins that approached and passed us, leaping above the water to the height of our deck. The final image is that of a young woman on whose naked breast a butterfly descended one day at noon while cicadas filled the air with their noise. This was for me another revelation of the mystery of light. It is a mystery which I think we Greeks can fully grasp and present. It may be something unique to this place. Perhaps it can be best understood here, and poetry can reveal it to the entire world. The mystery of light. When I speak of solar metaphysics, that's exactly what I mean.

I am not for the clarity of intelligence, that which the French call "la belle clarté." No, I think that even the most irrational thing can be *limpid*. *Limpidity* is probably the one element which dominates my poetry at present. The critic Varonitis has perceived this. He says that in my book "The Light Tree" there is an astonishing limpidity. What I mean by limpidity is that behind a given thing something different can be seen and behind that still something else, and so on and so on. This kind of transparency is what I have attempted to achieve. It seems to me something essentially Greek. The limpidity which exists in nature from the physical point of view is transposed into poetry. However, as I told you, that which is limpid can at the same time be altogether irrational. My kind of clarity is not that of the *ratio* or of the intelligence, not *clarté* as the French and Westerners in general conceive it.

You always look somewhat puzzled, I notice, whenever I contrast Greeks with Westerners or Europeans. This is not a mistake on my part. We Greeks belong politically, of course, to the Occident. We are part of Europe, part of the Western world, but at the same time Greece was never only that. There was always the oriental side which occupied an important place in the Greek spirit. Throughout antiquity oriental values were assimilated. There exists an oriental side in the Greek which should not be neglected. It is for this reason that I make the distinction.

Let me conclude by reading to you a concise statement I have prepared concerning the aims of my poetry:

> I consider poetry a source of innocence full of revolutionary forces. It is my mission to direct these forces against a world my conscience cannot accept, precisely so as to bring that world through continual metamorphoses more in harmony with my dreams. I am referring here to a contemporary kind of magic whose mechanism leads to the discovery of our true reality. It is for this reason that I

believe, to the point of idealism, that I am moving in a direction which has never been attempted until now. In the hope of obtaining a freedom from all constraints and the justice which could be identified with absolute light, I am an idolater who, without wanting to do so, arrives at Christian sainthood.

Translated from the French
By
Ivar and Astrid Ivask

Page 16: Four title illustrations for Elytis's books. *(Upper Left) Prosanatolizmí* (Orientations; 1967) by Tsaroúhis. *(Upper Right) To Axion Estí (The Axion Estí;* 1959) by Yannis Móralis. *(Lower Left) To fotódhendro ke i dhekáti tetárti omorfiá* (The Light Tree and the Fourteenth Beauty; 1971) by Ghika. *(Lower Right) Ta eterothalí* (The Stepchildren; 1974) by Ghika *(Photo: Ivar Ivask).*

Page 17: Page from the facsimile edition of Elytis's *To Monóghrama* (The Monogram), Cyprus 1971.

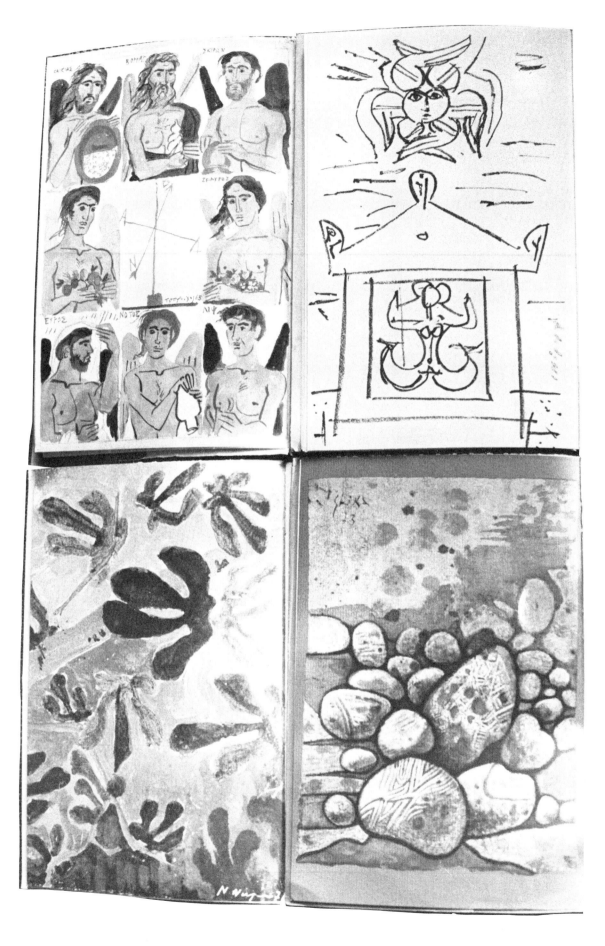

"Έχω δει πολλά και η γη μου απ' το νου μου
    φαίνεται ωραιότερη
Ωραιότερη μες στους χρυσούς ατμούς
Η πέτρα η κοφτερή ωραιότερα
Τα μπλάβα των ισθμών και οι στέρφε μες
    στα κύματα
Ωραιότερες οι αχτίδες όπου δίχως να πατείς
    περνάν
Αήττητη όπως η θεά της Σαμοθράκης πάνω
    από τα βουνά της θάλασσας

Έτσι ο έρως κοιτάζει που μου ζάρωσ'
Νάχει ο χρόνος δυο αδυνατεί
Μες στο αυλάκι που το πέρασμά σου θ' αφήνει
Σάν δελφίνι πρωτόπειρο ν' ακολουθεί

Και να παίζει με τ' άσπρο και το κυανό
    η ψυχή μου !

a short anthology
of translations from elytis's works

Four Poems from "Stepchildren" (1974)

By ODYSSEUS ELYTIS

Small Analogon for Nikos Hadjikyriákos-Ghika

Only so much
As is needed for the sea's roar to smooth a pebble
Or the sky's chill at daybreak to be incised
On the skin of a violet fig

And there
Far away on the promontory edge of Time
Where the bleak barren island is ravaged by the South Wind

Only so much even there: flourished the Invisible!

We however construct it, we however cultivate it
We however spin it out in stories night and day

And often at that time when earth
The Virgin
With the sun's acanthus and eyebrows firmly drawn

Ascends disentangled from the leprosy of continents

As in a dream, it is again we who offer it
One of us the stone, another the dew, another the day's rough cast

O earthen man

Behold what the night's confinement has brought
Cobalt and cinnebar, ink-black and ochre

Send your glance on high like an acute thought
To tear through the warring firmament

And say that we, the asymmetrical,

Are traces you pursued, left in the world's crannies
By the wild honeybees and the bereaving Lamb.

Mozart: Romance
(From the Concerto for Piano, Op. 20, K. 466)

Lovely saddening life
Piano distant and subterranean
My head leans on the Pole
And grass holds me in its dominion

Secret Ganges of the night where are you taking me?
I see roe-deer emerging from black smoke
Running in silver running
And I do not live and I have not died

Neither love not even glory
Nor was it even ever a dream
As on my side I am sleeping sleeping
I hear the machinery of the earth traveling.

Event in August

I went in circles around the sky and shouted

In danger of touching a happiness

I picked up a stone and aimed it afar.

Tipped off by the sun, Fate

Pretended not to see

And the girl's bird took a crumb of the sea and ascended.

The Leaf Diviner

This evening of August eight
My old house with its small lizards
Shipwrecked in the shallows of stars
And the melted candle wax on the night table
The doors and windows wide open
As my old house with its cargo
Of desolation enters into the night;

Bewildered voices and others still
Running through foliage flash
Like the secret passing of fireflies
From the depths of a life turned Up-
Side down in the cold whiteness of eyes
There where Time does not move
And the Moon with its cheek eaten away

Approaches my own in despair;
A dark rustling as from a lost
Love come back again. The voices begin:
"Don't." And then again "Don't." "My baby."
"What will your fate be?" "One day you'll remember this."
"Child my little child with your chestnut hair."
"I who love you." "Say always." "Always."

And yet into the greedy maw of the black
Garden that opens wide in two
All your possessions, but burnt
Out cinders, plunge submerged
As from the soul's waste waters a dull
Wave rises whose bubbles are
Just so many more old sunsets:

Windows trembling in the light of the evening star
A moment when you outstripped happiness
Like a song in which a girl brimming with tears
For your sake, hid for fear you'd see her—
All the sanctities of vows and embraces
Nothing nothing ever goes lost
This evening of August eight

Amid the greenery of sea-depths
That same interminable trembling again
Makes leaves rustle to themselves and to others
Speaks to itself in the Aramaic of a world apart:
"Child my little child with your chestnut hair
You were fated to be lost here and saved far away."
"You were fated to be lost here and saved far away."

And suddenly things future are seen like things past;
Traversable are all seas with their flowers
And I alone yet not alone; as always;
As when I was young and I walked on
With that place at my right side empty
And Vega following me in the heights above
The Patron Saint of all my loves.

Translated from the Greek
By
Kimon Friar

Picasso's Equivalences

By ODYSSEUS ELYTIS

Trying to follow closely the manner in which an artist develops the formal elements of his art, one frequently is led to the discovery of a certain "system of gestures." This system, which represents the reactions of its creator toward the surrounding world, can be transposed on a scale of spiritual values which will furnish us *through analogy* a table of multiple equivalences. Whether out-of-doors or in a studio, the artist is called upon to enact the same drama, always face-to-face with his destiny and with grand gestures ranging from triumph to despair.

One painter is a persecuted human being who shelters himself behind an existing piece of nature; another painter, in order to defend himself, proposes some pure tones which he has been able to extract, with the help of calculations, from a totality which does not cease to evade him. There are those who violently attack their own idol and remain would-be conquerors, returning with their hands full of derisory booty. Finally, there are the patient ones whose attentive fingers await the favorable moment which will permit them to unravel the famous Gordian knot of reality.

Amidst all these involuntary actors there suddenly appears Picasso with the look of Alexander the Great: the brush in his right hand has taken the place of the sword, and he opens his way and advances by cutting great swaths through reality. Because he knows that the most important thing is to advance. At every price and by whatever means except submission, compromise and blind obedience.

If a secret resists him, he attacks it by means of another. If an obstacle appears insurmountable, he transforms everything around this obstacle so that it no longer appears as such. This speed does not hurt him. It is his normal state, in which he can freely develop all his faculties and undertake those famous sharp turns at the end of which so many unsuspected aspects of reality are found forever fixed. This speed permits him also to reduce to a minimum the time required for action, the minimum that is needed for eye and heart to go together, beyond all calculations, to the discovery of the poetical interrelations of the world.

In this fashion, Picasso manages, one might say, to *disconcert* the nature of things. As if an object, familiar with the ways it has been approached for centuries, would do everything to persevere in its obstinacy not to reveal more than just a part of itself; yet suddenly encircled, attacked from all sides, not knowing where to flee (or, perhaps, as if weakening before a possible lover), it is forced to submit.

Thus, the most disobedient child of our age was needed to force concrete reality to obey it. It is in proportion to this disobedience that he offers us a new concept of reality. It is on account of this that he becomes the first realist of our age.

Let us retrace now the curve drawn by these bold and audacious lines; let us try to understand in our own way the order of these forms from which all attempts

This essay, originally written and published in French, is from Elytis's "Open Book" (Athens, Asterías, 1974, pp. 458–62).

at imitation have been excluded, yet from which, nevertheless, the semblances of the world gush forth with even greater vivacity: obviously a special kind of human behavior is implied in all this.

Isn't the painter who acts this way actually like somebody who, instead of accepting alms, affirms on the contrary his proud condition and *takes* that which he feels is his by right? Isn't he like a generous person who disdains to collect the interest which he could easily obtain from his possessions? In his domain, the creative act has long since replaced gold; he squanders his forces in making us partake of his riches. He does not think of himself. On the other hand, he also knows how to abandon the straight line, all the better to attain it, as a lover conquers his beloved using the only means by which she can be conquered. To affirm, as does the totality of his work, that the most fertile field for our imagination is not to be found in the sublime but rather among the most humble things which surround us, means to have confidence in life itself and its innumerable possibilities.

In the same way that the severe lines of a bare mountain, suggesting simplicity and leanness, evoke equivalent actions on the moral plane, so do the lines of Picasso, as he has developed them across the astonishing trajectory of his work, teach us the adventure and the enchanted discovery of the world and demand that we arrive at the realization of its poetical potential outside of all preconceived notions.

In spite of what has incessantly been claimed, Picasso has never cared to illustrate his epoch. He certainly has lived in close rapport with his times, but not in order to translate into artistic language the preoccupations in which it takes pride. The all too easy, seductive appeal of suffering, the idolization of that which is slightly sick, the exhibitionism of despair, the mysticisms/panaceas and the two-bit philosophies, all these spring forth from a spirit diametrically opposed to that which informs his very manner of drawing and painting. As a matter of fact, one is more inclined to believe, in view of recent works, that Picasso has wanted to *oppose* to the aberrations of his contemporaries something that is solid, a kind of physical and moral health which his passionate attachment to the search for truth has given him and which he probably considers the ultimate wisdom he has acquired in the course of his long career. He has never searched for Greece, but Greece has found him. Ever since that moment, it is the sea of the Golfe de Juan and the sun of Vallauris which have guided his steps. He speaks to us about the universe through his wife whom he loves and through his own children. He advances, his face parched by the sun, followed by the two archetypes which best represent his message: the pregnant woman and the famous goat.

Barely inside the refreshing shade of the Vallauris studios, one feels seized by the same gust of wind which, as often happens along the Mediterranean, makes the waters rise under a furious sun and fills up the deserted coast with all kinds of significant objects: an old burst basket, some bits of branches, an empty tin can, two half-broken pitchers. I was not at all surprised to discover these same objects, found by the artist in a carefree moment, solidly incorporated into his work, forming part of the flesh and bone of the forms built by the hands of the artist. A gesture which might have been mere playfulness attains in the work of Picasso the mysterious gravity of a ritual act, as if imposed by an unknown religion. This religion I have never been able to define myself, but it was familiar to me.

And all of a sudden I felt a fit of jealousy that these great symbols of the Mediterranean, these archetypes descended to us from time immemorial, were not created on one of the islands of the Aegean, where once upon a time the fingers of man, with a clumsiness that never lies, dared to shape matter. But this is of no importance; the lesson remains the same: it is sufficient to express that which we love, and this alone, with the fewest means at our disposal, yet in the most direct manner, that of poetry.

This poetical instinct, this building instinct par excellence, one finds again in the humble joy with which the fishermen build their boats or the villagers their houses. And this is how the works of this great man of the people appear to us: *useful* like boats or houses. We can inhabit their human warmth and let ourselves be carried by pointed prows toward the future. Contemplating these things, we gradually become aware of a realm where the idea of fecundity reigns, where the goat calls the hard rocks and the shrubs and the sea, a very simple world where one sees the big eyes of owls by night, and by day that row of pottery and tiles painted with a thousand faces which lead us from the multiplicity of the world back to its unique essence. Whether it is called "Vallauris" or "Human Dignity," this realm exists, offered to us once and for all, like a region of the soul where trickery is inconceivable, double-dealing impossible and flattery discouraged. Finally, it represents the marvelous equivalent of the means which Picasso uses to face his age, this extreme point where—let us dare to say it—the light of the sun and the blood of man are but one.

(1951)

Translated from the French
By
Ivar and Astrid Ivask

Selections from the "Open Book"

By ODYSSEUS ELYTIS

One does not renew oneself through love by renouncing women; one simply becomes a masturbator. And I believe that there is always more to learn from a virgin eye which has just returned from making the rounds of things familiar to us than from a common eye which has been privileged to wander in virgin territories. To understand this point, we only have to recall how Aragon of *Le paysan de Paris* saw a city, that had been described a thousand times, on the morrow of World War I and how the astronaut Leonov saw the unknown emptiness on the morrow of his exit into space.

It is the absence of imagination that changes man into a cripple unable to appreciate reality; and let practical men say what they may, men who one day depart from life without having even stammered it out are doubly ignorant. "La seule imagination me rend compte de ce qui peut être, et c'est assez pour lever un peu le terrible interdit."

And yet if you move from what is to what may be, you pass over a bridge which takes you from Hell to Paradise. And the strangest thing: a Paradise made of precisely the same material of which Hell is made. It is only the perception of the order of the materials that differs—one must imagine this in relation to the architectures of morality and feeling to understand—but this perception is nevertheless sufficient to determine the immeasurable difference. If reality, which is shaped by half of man's sensual and emotional dynamism, does not for the time being, and perhaps never will, allow the other architecture—or, putting it differently, the revolutionary re-creation—then the spirit stays free and, as I perceive it, remains the only thing which can undertake it. This is indeed the common characteristic that distinguishes the race of the poets: their separation from current reality. Beyond that, their manner of reaction—which also inevitably classifies them into separate groups—can for no reason whatsoever constitute a significant criterion.

My eyes were dazzled by the infinite gashes of the sun in the waves on a July midday; even if the olive groves did not exist I would have contrived them at such a moment; the same with the cicadas. In like fashion, I imagine, in another age, the world must have been created. And if it did not become better, it is undoubtedly because of man's fear to look at himself and to accept who he is before he speaks. I speak. I want to descend the steps, to fall into this flourishing fire and then to ascend like an angel of the Lord . . .

Ed. Note: This small anthology was selected and translated by Theofanis G. Stavrou in consultation with the poet.

The asynchronism of nature and man brought about the asynchronism of body and soul. Where nightingales are silent, Molotov cocktails are heard. Birds take vengeance. They never attended Sunday school. And young people, starting from Hungary or Sweden and reaching Czechoslovakia and France, seek through the cars which they overturn and the fires which they set, basically the rights of the black seed. It is imperative, since life cannot regress, that human beings progress even more, for fear that they might take it again, as someone could say, by its tail.

At the moment when the invisible but precisely for this reason more substantial and thrilling thaumaturgy continues in the form of a simple flower which opens its petals or of a sea which shines brilliantly in the sun, one has the right to hope that in the midst of formidable cyclotrons and electronic brains, some day just like between two Maltese stones, Poetry will shoot forth again like an all-red poppy. I am not talking about the ability to compose verses but, rather, the ability to re-create the world, literally and metaphorically, in such a way that the more the Poet's desires manage to materialize, the more they will contribute toward the realization of a Good acceptable by the totality of mankind. For a dreaming and chimerical Greek, which I do not hesitate to admit that I am, the meaning of this kind of Good cannot be in its final state anything but an ideal point, nevertheless made of soil and water, an "Island of the Blessed," not at all drowned in natural or some other kind of wealth, but moderate and demanding at the same time, like the Parthenon, naked and adapted to the golden slashing of the winds, with the whitewashed little wall of a church above the most dazzling sea.

I wrote because poetry begins from the point where the last word does not belong to death. It is the end of one life and the beginning of another, which is the same as the first one except that it goes very deep, to the most extreme point that the soul has managed to investigate, to the boundaries of the opposites where the Sun and Hades touch each other. It is the interminable course toward the light which is the Word and the Uncreated Light which is God.

A metaphorical summer was waiting for me, entirely the same, eternal, with the crackings of wood, the fragrances of wild herbs, the figs of Archilochos and the moon of Sappho. I was traveling as if I were walking in a diaphanous deep; my body was shining as green and blue currents were passing through it; I was caressing the speechless stone female figures, and in the reflections I was hearing by the thousands the chirpings of the glances; an endless row of ancestors, fierce, tortured, proud, moved each one of my muscles. Oh yes, it is not a small thing to have the centuries on your side, I kept saying all the time, and I went on.

Thus I passed through the indifferent "great public" and the "hostile Authorities," as I did through the Symplegades. And it is a lie that there is no Golden Fleece. Each

one of us is our own self's Golden Fleece. And it is a deception that death does not al-
low us to see it and recognize it. We must empty death from everything with which it
has been overstuffed, and reach it in absolute purity, in order to begin to distinguish
through it the true mountains and the true grass, the avenged world full of cool drops
which shine purer than the most precious tears.

This is what I await every year with one more wrinkle on my forehead and one
less wrinkle in my soul: the complete antistrophe, absolute diaphaneity. . . .

The grip of childhood years is, in the area of sensitivity, a demonic machine
whose dissolution, when the moment arrives, leaves us dumbfounded. Gradually, we
reach the point of not believing in ourselves for the sake of those who do not believe
—who do not want to believe—in their own selves. But then why do we write? Why
do we make poetry? I ask in the same manner that I would ask: Why do we make
love? On the cheeks of a girl as on the verses of a poem, from the sender to the re-
ceiver nothing mediates. The translation occurs without an interpreter and the gold-
dust which remains on our fingers looks sufficient. Nevertheless, if the wind blows
it again, the whole of nature will be inhabited by thousands of secret signs; and the
insatiable ghost which lies in wait inside us will open its mouth asking for more and
more.

As a whole, poets, musicians, artists, despite their great differences, and occasion-
ally thanks to them, in the depth and breadth of the ages constitute a second
state of the world. It is open to everyone, and there has not yet been found a military
demon strong enough to cut off the narrow streets. Only the access sometimes becomes
difficult, a difficulty corresponding to the degree of human stupidity. No one is obliged
to be interested in Poetry. Once he becomes interested, however, he is obliged to
"know how to move" in this second state, to walk both in air and on water.

When I had the opportunity for the first time to find myself on the deck of a ship
sailing south to Santorini, I had the feeling of a landlord surveying his ancestral estate
which he is about to inherit. These expanses curly with waves were the arable lands,
where all that had to be done was to plant cypress trees for boundary signs. I took
stock of my flocks. I owned my silos, my winepresses, my outbuildings. Neither did
I lack ships. On the hillside was the little monastery, there were two or three country
houses, and on the edge of the rock the pigeonholes and the mills. I felt pre-existing in
me an immense familiarity, which made me exchange with the greatest ease properties
and characters of things and which embellished all that the Atlantis of others had not
managed to drag with her into the deep.

If there were a way for someone to transcribe in visual symbols the kinetic phe-nomena which I felt taking place around me in that blinding golden blue space, he would have followed, by way of tracing the course from the sun to the roots of the plants and from the roots of the plants to the sun, the exchange between the properties of the herbs and the exhortations of men, the analogy between the exhortations of men and their daily objects, houses, boats, tools. And these he would have followed with so much clarity, consequence and frugality of means that their precise mo-ment he would have very soon been convinced could not be anything else but the only and ideal justice; because justice is a precise moment and nothing else.

Poetry is a mechanism that demechanizes man and his relations with things. The poet reaches the point where he goes into partnership with his own contradiction. On the level of language, the temptation for one to subject to a test the resistance of abnegation frequently leads him to a different type of acceptance. This is man, and what poet will dare define it? The truth remains to be discovered. In the meantime, let's talk about simpler things.

For me, in my youth, Greece was a dazzle. I have been neither a patriot nor a nature worshipper, or at least I experienced great surprise when I noticed that these qualities were attributed to me. Approximately what someone would have experienced in olden times if in the midst of storms he had suspected the existence of electricity and those around him had called him an autumn romantic.

During the years of Buchenwald and Auschwitz, Matisse painted the most juicy and unripe, the most charming flowers or fruits which were ever made, as if the very miracle of life had found a way to coil within them for good. That's why today they still speak more eloquently than the most macabre, cadaverous description of the period: because their creator refused to "punt" (may I be forgiven for this word) the so-called "feeling" and its homeopathic properties and preferred to obey not the phe-nomena but the reaction which such phenomena caused in his conscience.

A whole literature in our time has made the mistake of competing with the events, of going beyond them in presenting horror instead of counterbalancing it. But when the artistic word simply competes with the deed, it is as if it is asking to walk with the help of foreign crutches and to resemble a cripple because it has refused its own legs.

It is indeed strange what happens to man. It is difficult, impossible for him to be-lieve that what he imagines is identical with what he sees, and to admit that the nat-ural phenomena, too, are phenomena of the spirit. And he prefers to repeat twice the wretchedness of his life—once for his own sake and once for the sake of his art—instead of transforming it into some other, some different reality, creating, as we might say, from two certain deteriorations an eventual durability.

Primitive peoples, poets before the age of poems, not having at their disposal mirrors (literally and metaphorically) to behave in unseemly fashion, overcame evil by reciting frightful and incomprehensible words. In the same fashion, until a few years ago our island nurses, with utter seriousness, chased evil spirits from above our cradles by uttering words without meaning, holding a tiny leaf of a modest herb which received God knows what strange powers exclusively from the innocence of its own nature.

Poetry is precisely this tiny leaf with the unknown powers of innocence and the strange words which accompany it.

The fallacy was that we left [heroism] behind the door when the bells of peace tolled. The other half, the victors, turned it against other victors, so that we have had perpetual war on our hands. The only thing that we did not think of doing was to change its face, its panoply and its sword-edge, to transfer it—I mean heroism always—directly to the peaceful projects which were awaiting us, solid in the boldness and watchfulness of the soul, at the disposal of change and sacrifice. And yet from it societies expected not only their economic and administrative reorganization but, above all, their moral reform and biological revolution. Love, the senses, dreams were expiring from a new, unheard-of atrophy in the history of human imagination. And what else could the poet be at such moments but an oxygen donor? How else would he have felt that he was fulfilling his purpose other than by providing with his poems an example, by assuming legitimately the place vacated by the Robber, the Corsair, the Leader, the Conqueror or whatever, by continuing their active intervention into things, the accumulation of spoils and games, the discovery of unknown treasures, the annexation of territories distant and undiscovered.

Human units are like chemical elements. From their union result unanticipated powers capable of altering or corroding what up to that moment was considered unassailable to such a degree that one reaches the point of optimism that someday progress in the moral field, like that which is taking place in the scientific field today, will succeed in solving the world's problem. Alas. In this case, and despite deterministic theories, the great Chemist remains invisible, cantankerous, irrational. And just when you think that the moment for him to discover the secret powder of his soul has arrived, with one push he upsets all the sensitive instruments, shatters the glass tubes, mixes up the prescriptions in such a way that no one else can continue his work. And "the game for the game's sake" starts all over again. Let the wretched individual wait for his salvation. It is all over, finished; the hydrogen remains hydrogen and oxygen oxygen. They do not become water.

One step above the realization that Poetry is a simple confession, I could see the horizon changing, could see the whole landscape, just as from the top of one of our islands, where suddenly the familiar reliefs of the mainland change their shape and reveal to you unsuspected bays and promontories, distant backs of other islands, a new world, broader and richer in its variety. And the sieve of conscience you begin to discard and retain, retain and discard, until one day you feel yourself clear and diaphanous, such as all your secret inclinations wanted you to be and all conditions around you conspired to alter. It is difficult, so difficult to allow your epoch to set its seal on you without distorting you.

I demanded from the ideal poem that it consist of a miniature of a heliacal system, complete with the same tranquillity and the same expression of eternity in its totality, the same perpetual motion in its isolated component parts. Even today this is how I perceive the nuclear formation of a poem, like a closed unit, as well as its final self-powered centrifugation, always from the point of view of the meaning of the perceptible, which is consistently localized, isolated and illuminated by inspiration. The difference is that, in order to acquire substance and effectively replace the sun as well as fulfill its mission in the system of images and meanings which it carries along, it is imperative that this meaning develop uninterruptedly and parallel with a symbolic transcription of its own in signs of rhythmic and metrical weaving analogous to those which render the meaning of time sensible to human understanding.

I apologize for such a complex statement. I shall try to say it differently. The entire mechanism of the articulation of a calendar of holidays or of the mutual transmutation of natural and intelligible elements in a mythology must operate anew from the collective to the individual scale and through one means—the one and only means of lyrical action. Or, again, in other words: in each and every instance the development which is defined and the distribution of meanings must dictate a definite development and distribution of the parts; and, simultaneously, such a development and distribution of the parts must constitute a sine qua non of the fullness of the result.

Beyond that point, we can say that the place of the sun in the moral world plays the same role that it does in the nature of things. But the poet is a cutting edge of the moral and the real world. The part of the darkness which is neutralized within him, because of his conscience, is added onto a light which repeatedly returns to him in order to render constantly purer his idol, man. If there is a humanistic view about the mission of Art, this, I believe, is the only way it can be understood: like an invisible operation, which is a facsimile of the mechanism we call Justice—and naturally I am not talking about the Justice of the courts but about the other Justice, which is consummated slowly and equally painfully in the teachings of the great magistrates of mankind, in the political struggles for social liberation and in the loftiest poetic accomplishments. From such a great effort, the drops of light fall slowly every now and then into the vast night of the soul like lemon drops into polluted water.

The poet must be generous. Not wishing to lose even a moment from your supposed talent is like not wishing to lose even a drachma from the interest of the small capital donated to you. But Poetry is not a bank. On the contrary, it is the conception which actually opposes the bank. If it becomes a written text communicable to others, so much the better. If not, it does not matter. That which must happen and happen uninterruptedly, endlessly, without the slightest irregularity, is anti-servility, irreconcilability, independence. Poetry is the other face of Pride.

Translated from the Greek
By
Theofanis G. Stavrou

From the "Book of Signs"

By ODYSSEUS ELYTIS

Perfection has no Achilles' heel.

The Law which I am will not subdue me.

Dear God, how much blue do you squander that we may not behold You!

Far away, in the far depths of the Lamb, the battle rages.

Infinity is to us as language to the deaf-mute.

Between Tuesday and Wednesday your real day must have been mislaid.

The children and grandchildren of renunciation are all of them bastards.

In the village of my tongue Sorrow is called Luminous.

When calamity is to our advantage, then think of her as a whore.

Give away time as a gift if you wish to retain a little dignity.

Translated from the Greek
By
Kimon Friar

(Upper Left) Elytis, Athens 1931: Time of his first poems; *(Upper Right)* At the Albanian front 1941; *(Lower Half)* Congress of International Association of Art Critics, Paris 1949 (Elytis in center, behind desk plate of Greece).

(Upper Left) Chicago 1961;
(Upper Right) Cyprus 1970;
(Lower Half) Paris 1971.

(Upper Left and Right) Elytis in his Athens apartment 1974; *(Lower Half)* Autographing books in a Stockholm bookstore, December 1979 *(Photo: Lütfi Özkök).*

Elytis on 22 April 1975 at Tériade's Villa Natacha, Saint-Jean-Cap-Ferrat *(Photo: Ivar Ivask)*.

Elytis receiving the 1979 Nobel Prize for Literature from King Carl XVI Gustaf in Stockholm on 10 December 1979 *(Photo: Swedish Press)*.

critical perspectives

The Poetry of Elytis

By LAWRENCE DURRELL

There is no easier way to damn a poet than to call him "a poet's poet," and this has so frequently happened to Odysseus Elytis that it is time to insist on the accessibility of his work, on its timeliness and relevance to ourselves. His language is so choice, his range of metaphor so large, that he has presented quite a task to his translators. He has a romantic and lyrical mind which deploys a metaphysic of complete intellectual sensuality—the rocks, the islands, the blue Greek sea, the winds; they are at once "real" and also "signatures" in the alchemical sense. He makes his magic with them, and it is peculiarly Greek magic that he makes. Using the most up-to-date methods in technique, he has, at the same time, insisted that at bottom poetry is not simply a craft or a skill but an act of divination. His poems are spells, and they conjure up that eternal Greek world which has haunted and continues to haunt the European consciousness with its hints of a perfection that remains always a possibility. The Greek poet aims his heart and his gift directly at the sublime—for nothing else will do. That is why we respond with ardour and wonder when we see a poet like Elytis taking the same path as the ancients, and at his best, joining forces with them to affirm the eternal Mediterranean values of his land and tongue. How lucky, too, that he has found in Kimon Friar a translator who can transplant his poetry into English, so that its freshness and spontaneity still shock and delight.

Eros: His Power, Forms and Transformations in the Poetry of Odysseus Elytis

By ANDONIS DECAVALLES

> I have conceived my figure between a sea that comes to view right behind the whitewashed little wall of a chapel and a barefoot girl with the wind lifting her dress, a chance moment I struggle to capture, and I waylay it with Greek words.
>
> If I spoke at the beginning about a girl and a chapel, at the risk of sounding less than serious, I had my reasons. I would have liked to draw that girl into the chapel and make her my own, not to scandalize anyone, but to confess that the eros is one, and also to make more dense the poem I wish to make out of the days of my life.
>
> I would then see pomegranate branches sprouting from the iconostasis, and the wind singing at the little window together with the sea-wave, when the South Wind, blowing stronger, would help that wave jump over the stone parapet. Once, such a parapet touched my naked body, and I felt my innards purified, as if the lime, with its disinfectant qualities, had passed through all the folds of my heart. This is why I was never afraid of the wild look of the Saints, like anybody who ever reached the inapproachable. I knew that I was just enough to decode the Laws of my imaginary republic and to reveal that that was the seat of innocence. Do not take this as arrogance. I do not speak about myself. I speak for anyone who feels like myself but does not have enough naïveté to confess it.
>
> If there is, I think, for each one of us a different, a personal Paradise, mine should irreparably be inhabited by trees of words that the wind dresses in silver, like poplars, by men who see the rights of which they have been deprived returning to them, and by birds that even in the midst of the truth of death insist on singing in Greek and on saying "eros, eros, eros!"

("Open Book," pp. 39–42)

To speak of Eros in Elytis's poetry, Eros in the fullness of his meaning, is tantamount to excluding very little. Elytis the poet has been above all Elytis the lover of the beauty in his "girls" and in nature, particularly that Aegean world of purity, serenity and love. He has been the lover of life and its poetry, of the tangibles and the intangibles, of earth and its ascent to the sky, and has ultimately been forced to become the passionate defender of them all. Eros has been the force that has driven both his life and pen, the earthly yet transcending power that has aspired to accomplishing the happy marriage of earth and heaven. We cannot afford not to think of Blake, his innocence, his experience and his eventual marriage of heaven and hell. Elytis's progress has been identical, even to the point of his turning himself into the prophet of a new Paradise. Their differences lie, of course, in their different times and worlds. In the place of Blake's northern New Jerusalem there is Elytis's sun-drenched Aegean, the day and its light, the summer and its noon and a youth that never ends. Much like Blake, Elytis shaped his own personal myth. Onto his pagan and Christian inheritances, the coexistent and inseparable products of the same racial genius, the same frame of mind, he put his own creative stamp. With the exception of the all-ruling sun, his divinities have stayed nameless in an animistic world. They are the natural and the inner forces that once gave birth to ancient myth.

The passage quoted above, a retrospective self-portrait, contains almost the entire essence of Elytis. Commenting and expanding on its parts, we could give a picture of the whole; for Elytis, like most significant poets and creators, has had one basic story to tell, the progressive story of Eros's nature, his longings, his advancement and conquests and his external and internal discoveries in the process of building a world at once natural, human, esthetic, earthly and universal, timely and timeless, finite and infinite, mortal yet immortal. The taking of that girl into that whitewashed chapel by the sea brings together the pagan and the Christian worlds in the purity of the erotic act, with Dionysian pomegranates of fertility and ecstasy sprouting from the iconostasis. It is this purity which counts, the sacredness of Eros, the transformation of what was wrongly deemed sin into virtue, Arete, and the concomitant raising of the earth to the heights of the sky or heaven (the Greek *ouranós* means both). In the process the poet-lover is not frightened by the wild-looking, ossified faces of the saints. Those faces, after all, have in them the familiarity of the barren and rocky Greek soil.

Our gothic century has not ingratiated us with beauty. Beauty has long been out of fashion and respect, much as has been goodness, the other half of that blessed ancient couple, *kalón* and *agathón*. We have long abided with the anguished Baudelairean version of beauty, and it is certainly a solace to witness in Elytis a rejuvenation of that old pair under the cascading light of a sovereign sun, to rediscover an Eros of beauty in both matter and spirit, in both body and soul. A declared Platonist, Elytis, in his own manner, has stood faithfully by Diotima's words, yet with a slight but significant difference. If, for the somewhat dualistic Diotima, the beauty of the body was there to lead the way to the beauty of the soul, the same is true for Elytis; but the body is not left behind. The two types of beauty exist as one.

Who have been the lovers in Elytis, his erotic males and females? The dominant lover has certainly been the poet himself, representing as well all the honest lovers of his kind, the human and the elemental. His universal alter ego has been the sun, a sun that stood active on both sides of Plato's divided line. And how else could it be in a world primarily visual, one of images, of parallels embracing in a constant fruitional and fructifying exchange? As for his beloved ones, we have mentioned the "girls"—for the most part anonymous, archetypal, occasionally called Myrto (for the myrtle and its sexual connotation in one of Archilochus's fragments), or Marina for her sea association, or Helen or Eva. Other lovers, alternating with the girls, are the sea, the mother earth, the boats, the pomegranate trees, the islands (Santorini above all), Greece, a "sunray" in "her" variations of colors, "drops of pure water" turning into maids (Arete is one of them), the Virgin Mary as Panayia or Evangelistra (Our Lady of the Annunciation) or the Unfading Rose, and incarnated abstractions such as Hope, Purity, Freedom and the Platonic Ideas.

No short survey could adequately cope with the immense variety of Eros's pervasive presence in Elytis's work. As we enter his world, Eros or "Erotas" greets us from the opening page, as the initial word in the very first of his "First Poems" in the collection "Orientations," the poem entitled "Of the Aegean." Here Eros is framed by the standard elements of his setting:

Love
The archipelago
And the prow of its foam
And the seagull of its dream

.   .   .   .

Love
Its song
And the horizons of its voyage
And the echo of its nostalgia

.   .   .   .

Love
Its ship
And the freedom from care of its etesian winds
And the jib of its hope

.   .   .   .

(*SS*, p. 47)*

The only sorrow that at times reaches this early, erotic world of Elytis, the only "cloud" of darkness upon it, is the absence of the beloved, as in the "Climate of Absence," with its "knot of sorrow" and the torment of memory. But even here "hope" is always present to disperse the sadness with happiness and fulfillment.

Widely known and very popular among Elytis's earliest poems has been the epigrammatic, Platonic quatrain in which the girl grows as an incarnation of Ideas: "Prior to my eyes you were the light / Prior to Eros you were Eros himself / And when the kiss took you / You became Woman." The same motif is repeated in the "Windows to the Fifth Season," wherein the poet says of the girl, "How beautiful she is! She has taken on the form of that thought which feels her when she feels it devoted to her." (*SS*, p. 49) As for the power of the erotic embrace: "Two arms are waiting. An entire earth supports itself on their elbows. An entire poetry on their expectation." (*SS*, p. 50) And then, as if in sympathetic magic, nature is creatively affected by the girl's beauty: "In the touch of your palms the fruit will repose that hovers now without purpose. In the translucent abutment of your body's stature, trees will find the long-lived fulfillment of their whispered isolation. In your first freedom from care herbs will multiply like hopes. Your presence will cool the dew." (ibid.) As for Eros himself, the creator, he too has to be given form: "And when the sky runs under the bridges of our woven hands ... we shall create the form of love lacking from these visions / It is then we shall / To the ritual of difficult dreams a sure restoration." (ibid.) In the later works *The Axion Esti* and the "Six and One Remorses for the Sky" the dreams will be restored to "take their revenge upon reality."

Eros aspires to rise, to ascend to sky/heaven—a transcendence which finds its earliest, fullest, most traditional, most Platonic-Dantesque version in the early "Orion," one of Elytis's very few night poems. Let us notice, by the way, that in contrast to most love poets Elytis is a daytime, noontime lover. In "Orion" the world comes to terms with bitterness as night falls and is liberated from noise and worry. "Our head is in the hands of God." A prayer transforms the heights, we become "the

*The designation *SS* will be used throughout this article to refer to Odysseus Elytis, *The Sovereign Sun*, Kimon Friar, tr. Philadelphia, Temple University Press, 1974. The notation *AE* will be used to refer to Elytis's *The Axion Esti*, Edmund Keeley and George Savidis, trs., Pittsburgh, University of Pittsburgh Press, 1974. Quotations cited without reference to either of these two works are my own translations from the Greek.

descendants of the perishable tears," we leave behind us our earthly skin, and "our foreheads neighbor the stars." A shower of light dresses every notion in the air, which brings our "hope" closer to serenity. Our souls advance to their meeting with heaven. The pure moment shines. Within us "silence is dissolved," and memory rolls into "an uninhabited chaos, when we granted ourselves to an unbelievable shore, a shore of light shades, once dreamed of through tears . . . We detached ourselves from our weight as we detached ourselves from sin." Our new dream "palpitates pure. An invisible hand pulls our own to where Calm becomes an innocent heaven where the soul masters itself unchangeable."

Furtively present in several of Elytis's early love poems is a sense of sin, sin which is to be purified. As if to cancel the quasi-metaphysical, traditionally spiritual ascent in "Orion," the poet in his "Anniversary" poem posits an earthly, a marine paradise within human, earthly access "Where a man may go / Who is nothing else but a man." The poet himself brought his life "To this spot that struggles / Always near the sea / Youth on rocks, breast / To breast against the wind" to grow there from childhood to manhood and to learn from the elements, where "A few years, a few waves" are a "Sensitive rowing / In the bays surrounding love." (*SS*, p. 61) It should be noticed that here as well as in several other instances, youth and erotic growth, erotic adolescence and its earthly teleology involve a sea-journey, on which the poet-lover, "a stone pledge to the watery element," sails "Further off than the islands / Lower than the waves," where "hope is resplendent with all its dolphins / The sun's gain in a human heart" and where the eyes can certainly uphold "infinity." (ibid., p. 62)

In its concern for the heights and depths in the erotic sea-journey of exploration and discovery, "The Clepsydras of the Unknown" prophesies a union of opposites, a constant, insistent Heraclitean/neo-Platonic expectation: "A day will come when the cork will imitate the anchor / and will steal the taste of the deep / A day will come when their double self will be united." In moments of quandary the poet painfully wonders what might be the key of that "other gate," the gate to that "other world." Is it Eros? Life is certainly measured with pulses, joy and "desperate gesticulations." Toil is needed. Youth passes, despair prevails, but there also comes the promise of sunrise to discard darkness. Merry lips kiss girls, a boat sets sail full of songs, and there are "marble mansions of naked women / Each one of them was once a drop of water / Each one now is light." Swarms of erotic visions follow: "Earth is simple and leading / Layers of kindness, one by one, like florins cut in the sun / in the lips, in the teeth, one by one, the sins / Of life are peeled into goods." Noon brings callings of purity; the poet is ready "to go out to the white gates of noon, to ring with voices the blue bells of resurrection / And all the cold islands will set their hair afire and promenade / With innocent flames and pebbles the erotic open seas." The day, then, whose "nocturnal past" is "purified" by the dawn, comes into its full glory. "Darkness owes me light," the poet exclaims, contemplating the "Blond day, reward of the sun and of eros." Twenty-one short subsequent pieces, under the title "Serenities," are "earthly fragments of happiness," poems of love, of admiration and praise of girls and nature in their mutual exchange and fruition that render Death "useless."

In contrast to the Apollonian clarity and equanimity of "Anniversary" and "The Clepsydras," the orgiastic "Dionysus" brings a high sensualism, lust, inebriation and frenzy, and teems with monsters and wild beasts. This is one of Elytis's richest pieces, one of Asiatic splendor, with its "swift schooners of desire," with the expectations of "eternity" in sight, with women that "beautify clarity," with rainbows sailing through crystal skies and sending amber boats down to earth.

In the longish "Concert of the Hyacinths" we overhear the intimate whisperings, the complaints and admonitions, of a lover to his beloved. He is her initiator into the world of Eros and its mysteries. This and other early poems by Elytis bring to mind the "carpe diem" tradition, yet without the traditional simplicity that reached its highest sophistication in John Donne. The lover's complaint here concerns his beloved's dangerous playfulness, her high airs, her irresponsibility, her remoteness and her disregard of the value and depth of his feelings and of her own power. "You leave and disappear, conquering your presence, creating a divine solitude, a turbulent and incomprehensible happiness . . . I did nothing else but what I found and imitated in You!" He proclaims her "the only reality," but hastens to add, "When you leave those who are assimilated within nonexistence and offer yourself again as a mortal woman, I awaken in your transformation from the beginning . . . Do not play any longer. Cast the ace of fire. Break open the human geography." (SS, pp. 53–58)

"Sun the First" came out in 1943, during the time of the Nazi Occupation of Greece, when the war experience was already past. Might we assume that the poems in this book were conceived in an earlier day? Or were they a reaction to darkness with recollected light? War does not appear in them, nor does its ugly immediate aftermath; but there is, to some extent, a maturity born of the Greek war experience, an awareness of suffering in life and of the need to transcend that suffering. Eros in these poems widens his embrace beyond the Aegean innocence to reach a world less private. The cure for evil lies in the recollection of that bright Aegean sun. As if in retrospect, the poet says:

> I spoke of love, of the rose's health, the sunray
> That alone finds the heart straightway
> Of Greece that walks the sea with surety
> Of Greece that takes me on voyages always
> To naked snow-glorious mountains
>
> I give my hand to justice
> Translucent fountain, spring on the mountain summit
> My sky is deep and unchanging
> Whatever I love is born unceasingly
> Whatever I love is always at its beginning.
> (SS, p. 76)

Wasn't Ezra Pound, too, to exclaim in Pisa, "What thou lovest well remains"? Justice and heroic Greece herself now enter the gallery of Elytis's loved ones. The closer familiarity with suffering and pain, even death, evokes a greater effort from Eros. "Pain rounds the good cape / No voice gets lost in the bays of the sky."

In an art that had achieved a better mastery of its means through compact simplicity and meaningful selectivity, the poems in "Sun the First" reproduce in a more sculpturesque manner the quintessence of the Aegean world found in "Orientations." The love of a girl and of nature brings the poet to enter the surrounding procreative processes more deeply. He becomes another element, a driving force, to fructify and aid the world creatively, to help it achieve its physical and supernal function, its destination and rebirth. Negatives are turned into positives ("I know the night no longer that is a night only" [*SS*, 75]), and inimical elements are now viewed as contributory to that creation in which Eros is the primum mobile. Yeats's "Adam's Curse" comes to mind as we read the concluding poem of this group: "With what stone, what blood, what iron / What fire we are made." We poets, says Elytis, may be called idealists, woolgatherers or visionaries when "our arms open under an all-white Idea" which we entreat but which "never descends." However, "the desire's vision wakes up in flesh one day / And where, before, a naked wilderness shone / A City is now laughing, as beautiful as you wanted it." This initial plea for the poet-creator was eventually to develop into a passionate self-defense in Elytis's later poetry.

Closer to his erotic theme and very ingeniously conceived is the seven-poem sequel to "Sun the First" entitled "Variations on a Sunbeam." The "Variations" are the colors of the spectrum, slightly shuffled in their order and increased in number from six to seven—Elytis's ever-present mystical number (there are seven heavens in Greek tradition)—to serve his symbolism. The colors of the sunray, we easily realize, are the seven stages of the day from dawn to evening; but they are also the seven stages in a girl's erotic experience and growth, from the birth of Eros in her virginal girlhood to his decline at the end of her youth. The "red" is for her lips: "Your mouth speaks with four hundred roses / Beats the trees, raptures all the earth / Pours into her body the first shuddering." The "green" represents physical greenness or immaturity, "the girl who has not yet entered eros fully / But keeps in her apron an acrid grove of fruit"; the lover tells her: "My girl / I have an untouched grass in my heart / A rain of newborn trefoil / And a cascade that has not yet pounced / It lies deeper, lower, it will pounce / Like a wild beast of day upon your April." The "yellow" is that of the day as it approaches fullness, of girls with uncovered breasts that "Go and blow gibbets of fire with trumpets in the threshing floors / Burn hay, melt gold coins . . ." We reach the climax when the girl, inebriated by the sun, consents to be called the "Orange Girl" and is surrounded by the "seven heavens glittering" and by crystals and swallows. Her inebriation seizes the vine, the heron and the whole world, all of them whispering her secret name further and further. She is now told that "No one knows you as the kiss does." Through the "light blue" color of her eyes the poet contemplates the sky, the stars and Hope, in an ascent to the heights; and the "deep blue," being the color of infinity, indicates the depths revealed. The wind acquires deep-blue lips, the girl's glance grows endless, the blue of the sea becomes a revealing light, and the poet sees "a deep-colored bird drunk with the riddle of her embrace." The cycle closes with a Baudelairean "violet," the mournful color of the evening and of death.

One would not expect the erotic element to have a major part in the "Heroic and Elegiac Song for the Lost Second Lieutenant of the Albanian Campaign" (1945). The theme here is the acquaintance with, the knowledge, conquest and transcendence of death. The brilliant Aegean is for the hero a world now lost but affectionately recollected, a solace in the midst of suffering. The hero was indeed a lover once: "Love was so huge within him," and "In the arms of bitter-orange girls at night / He would soil the large garments of the stars." (*SS*, p. 91) Yet even the hero's ascent to heaven in part XII has an erotic touch in an idealistic, solemn sense. Eros again enhances the ascent: "With a morning stride on the growing grass / He ascends alone and blazing with light . . . / Flower tomboys wave to him secretly / And speak to him in high voices that turn to mist on the air / Even the trees bend toward him lovingly" (ibid., p. 95); and the crystal bells tolling in part XIII "tell of him who burned in life / . . . / who was not given time to weep / For his deep longing for the Love of life." (ibid., p. 96) The last part, a Gloria, with a vision of Liberty shining in the firmament, trans-forms the erotic aspect: "Rainbow-beaten shores fall into the water / Ships with open sails voyage on the meadows / The most innocent girls / Run naked in men's eyes / . . . / He is continually ascending; / Around him those passions glow that once / Were lost in the solitude of sin." (SS, pp. 96–97) The Liberty that the hero's sacrifice accomplishes brings a purification of passions, along with a resurrection and a life reborn.

It took several years of silence, meditation and study for that rebirth to find its elements and form. A poetic "genesis" was needed, however, if that life was to rise from darkness into life again, a recollection, an introspection, a sense that the restora-tion of things lost would be worth our effort, our love and our praise, worth our life. This restoration required a deeper awareness of all that was involved. Eros, above all else, was again the Demiurge, and *The Axion Esti* (1959) is, in fact, an account of Eros's doings: his shaping the world anew; his battle with hatred, enmity, misun-derstanding and their darkness; his victory, justification and praise. Like the biblical God, the poet-lover is the vocal shaper of the Aegean universe as a world without and a world within, physical and spiritual, a microcosm that is a macrocosm, "THIS WORLD / this small world the great!" Platonically, the poet is "still tied to heaven." (*AE*, p. 3) He identifies himself as "the One I really was, the One of many centuries ago / the One still verdant in the midst of fire" (we get here a triple reference: to Plotinus, to the burning bush in which God appeared to Moses on Mt. Sinai, and of course to Greece's eternal youth despite her age), and he creates in obedience to the sun, whose axis is in him and whose voice, like Fate above the poet's crib, comes "like memory become the present," like Hesiod's and Plato's Mnemosyne. The world to be created is "written" in the poet's entrails and thus takes form as a self-projection. And since creation is a battle against chaos in which one is to use "his own weapons," the poet's weapons at the outset are "Pomegranates or Zephyrs or Kisses."

Light is already present when the earth is created, first as a female, as a woman's naked body shaped in an erotic embrace: "the curves gentle / one inside the other / *land masses that made me feel / the smell of earth like understanding*." (*AE*, p. 5) The constant exchange in later Elytis, the interfusion of the concrete with the abstract, of the esthetic with the ethical, of the physical with the mental, the deeper common identity of *kalón* and *agathón*, presents us with a moment of joyous exultation as the poet-creator shapes and populates the earth:

> There, alone, he placed
> > white marble fountains
> > mills of wind
> > tiny pink cupolas
> > and tall perforated dovecotes

Virtue with its four right angles
And since he thought it beautiful for each to be in another's arms
            the large watering troughs filled with love
            the cattle lowered their heads, gently, calves and cows
            as though the world held no temptations
            as though knives were yet unknown

                                                        (*AE*, p. 7)

Eros with its purity in an Eden.

The sea is created next and is likewise a female, the equivalent of purity, "innocent and tremulous like a vineyard / deep and unscarred like the sky's other face, / *A drop of soul amidst the clay*." (*AE*, p. 9) And in the midst of the sea he plants the islands, "little worlds in [his] image and likeness." The names of the plants and herbs he creates next are "*Secret syllables through which I strove to utter my identity*." The sun tells him at this point: "Good, . . . you know how to read / and you'll come to learn a great deal / if you study the Insignificant in depth" (*AE*, p. 11), echoing Blake's "To see a World in a Grain of Sand."

Next the girls are created, shaped in the image of "red jugs lined up on the quay / . . . / Maidens beautiful and naked and smooth like pebbles / with that touch of black in the delta of the thighs / . . . / some upright sounding the Conch / others spelling out in chalk / words strange and enigmatic: / ROES, ESA, ARIMNA / NUS, MIROLTAMITY, YELTIS" (*AE*, p. 13), anagrams of Eros, Sea, Marina, Sun, Immortality and Elytis—in short, no less than the essentials of the poet's erotic-spiritual paradise.

Wilderness, too, will have to be encountered, conquered, made fertile and thereby transcended: "But first you will see the wilderness and give it your own meaning . . . / The wilderness will precede your heart / and then again the wilderness will follow it." (*AE*, p. 15) In the process, positives need to be drawn out of negatives: "night after night / *I sought whiteness to the utmost intensity / of blackness, hope to the point of tears / joy to the outer limit of despair*." Through this ascetic exercise purity is reached, purity that is "the same on the slopes as in your entrails"; and as the sun heats mint, lavender, verbena, his "light threads of silver / falling from the heights" become the "cool hair of a girl I saw and wanted / Tangible woman / 'Purity,' he said, 'is she' / and full of yearning I caressed the body / kisses teeth to teeth; then one inside the other." (*AE*, p. 17) Eros with Purity, and in that embrace Good and Evil meet at a point reminiscent of Eliot's "still point of the turning world."

Finally, necessity, too, the "other element," the "monstrous Duty" with its "four voids," the concern for the other people, the experience with the "black men," the enemies, would have to be confronted, accepted, understood and transcended by the Sun of Justice that becomes human, becomes the poet himself. "Necessity" is that which takes us into the second section of *The Axion Esti*, "The Passion"—the poet's and the world's war experience which turned the poet into a fighter and eventually a missionary of his world and message. In darkness and suffering, the soul, taken unawares, is temporarily disoriented, until it discovers the redeeming value of its experience. In his loneliness the poet sings of himself as a single swallow still unable to bring in the difficult spring. There is fighting on the mountains and fighting at sea, where, miraculously, however, "Small craft rounding the cape / suddenly turn over and vanish, / emerge again among the clouds / on the other side of the deep." (*AE*,

p. 57) In this small craft's re-emergence is symbolized the spirit of an entire people, the brave fighters conquering death with death, and of the poet's own spirit in a pattern of death and resurrection so prominent in Elytis. At the center of it all, the poet wonders where he can find his "soul, the four-leaf tear" (*AE*, p. 63) and appeals to the "Intelligible sun of Justice" (recalling Plato's *Republic*?) not to forget his country.

Several parts of this section of *The Axion Esti* turn into a passionate self-defense by the poet against the charges of the "young Alexandrians":

> "Look," they said, "the naive tourist of the century—
>   so insensitive:
> when the rest of us mourn, he rejoices
>
> . . . .
>   A man with no friend
> or follower,
>   who trusts his body only
> and looks for the great mystery inside the sun's thorny leaves,
>   this is he,
> the outcast of the century's marketplaces!
>
> . . . .
>   The antichrist and callous satanist of the century!"
>   (*AE*, p. 71)

Possessed of a world view diametrically opposed to the modern existential anguish, Elytis has been attacked by those who have failed to see the depth below his surface, to realize his tragic awareness and the world-redeeming qualities of his Eros and his Purity. As Plato himself believed, one does not cure evil with evil, nor sorrow with sorrow. The noblest remedy is Eros, Love. Recollecting his youth, the poet exclaims:

> Good for you, my first youth and untamed lip,
> You who taught the storm's pebble
>   and in the midst of squalls talked back to the thunder
>
> . . . .
> I'm clean from end to end.
>   and in the hands of Death a useless vessel,
> bad prey in the claws of the brutal.
>   (*AE*, p. 87)

He laments the loss of that youth, and his voice grows softer and nostalgic in what sounds like a love complaint to God, he tells Him how to His creation he brought lasting Rose" (*AE*, p. 97), that quintessence of virginal girlhood and femininity as well, which has always been more human, more intimate and accessible to the Greek Orthodox Christian than the awesome and remote Holy Trinity. Then, in what sounds like a love complaint to God, he tells Him how to His creation he brought his own, as a gift to a gift, but that God's creation, with the element of evil contained in it, destroyed the poet's creation, his pure world of dream.

> I ROUSED the sensual pleasures early,
>
> . . . .
> I flung the darkness on the bed of love
>   with worldly things naked in my mind,
>
> . . . .
> and once again gave birth to the visible.
>   (*AE*, p. 101)

God's response is a restoration: "You blew and my entrails yearned, / one by one the birds came back to me!" The recovery ushers in a new joy with which the earthliness

of the Aegean world rises now to a quasi-metaphysical level, from mortality to deifica-
tion, where the poet assumes an almost sacred mission to serve what is new, to wor-
ship the innocent, the naked, the virginal creatures. His chastity will have the "purity
of the instinct" of reproduction, ready to pass the test of sin, which in turn will be
purified. There the "eleventh Commandment" will emerge from his eyes: "Either
this world or none other shall be." (*AE*, p. 103)

The prose "Prophetic" that follows foretells of the time when "Many years after
Sin—which they called Virtue in the churches and gave it their blessing—and after
the storm—which will be given birth by the mind of man—will have swept relics of
old stars and cobwebbed corners of the heavens, then Creation . . . shall shudder."
Hades shall be shaken by the sun, a sign that "the time has come for dreams to take
their revenge." (*AE*, p. 105) This ascent, this glory, must first be preceded by a descent
into the abyss of darkness. The "way up" will follow the "way down." First, "beauty
will be surrendered to the flies of the Marketplace." The men of power will be de-
throned, and against all will sail forth "the gunboats of Love." And in the superb
and inspired conclusion, the poet foresees the coming of new creators to a new Eden.

> And then the last of men will say his first word: that the grass shall grow tall and
> that woman shall rise at his side like a sun's ray. And again he will worship the
> woman and lay her upon the grass, as was ordained. And dreams will take their
> revenge, and they will sow generations forever and ever.
>
> (*AE*, pp. 107–109)

The "Meadows of Bliss" will eventually appear, emerging from the breast of the poet
himself, who will then advance into "a far and sinless country," accompanied by airy
creatures with trees walking by his side, a world of transcendence where, like Christ
returning to Jerusalem, he will be welcomed with "Hosanna to the coming one!" and
proclaimed "holy, holy / He, the conqueror of Hades and the savior of Eros" (*AE*,
pp. 113–15), for

> Now it is the hand of Death
>   that grants the gift of Life
> and sleep does not exist
> . . . .
> Forever forever and now and now the birds sing
>   PRAISED BE the price paid.
>
> (*AE*, p. 115)

The third and final section of *The Axion Esti* is its triumphant "Gloria," a hymn
to all the elements that compose the new Paradise, the things worthy of praise, all set
in a piece of exquisite beauty and harmony of imagery, music and symbolic devices.
We would naturally again expect the position and role of Eros to be central in this
creation of an ideal-yet-earthly world out of the insignificant yet beautiful things in
nature and in man, this union of the physical with the spiritual, of the earthly with
the universal. This hymn to an earthly heaven is interspersed with salutations to the
Girl, the Female and femininity, echoing the Orthodox Church's "Salutations" to
the Virgin in the Mass of "The Akathist Hymn": "Hail Girl Burning and hail Girl
Verdant / Hail Girl Unrepenting, with the prow's sword / . . . / Hail O Wild One of
the depth's paradise / Hail O Holy One of the islands' wilderness." (*AE*, pp. 125–27)
Particularly expressive is the passage delineating the archetypal variety of femininity:

THE GIRLS, blue grass of utopia
the girls, those Pleiades led astray
    the girls, those Vessels of the Mysteries
full to the brim yet bottomless

Astringent in the dark yet marvelous
carved out in light yet all darkness
    turning on themselves like a lighthouse
the sun-devouring, the moon-walking
                            (*AE*, p. 133)

Light is praised, human creation, the power of the sun, the islands, the sea, the winds, the house on the shore, sun's inebriation, noon, sleep, love, the girls, marriage, family, the living and the dead—in short, all things of the "now," which are also the things "forever." (*AE*, p. 147)

Contemporary with, and in a sense parenthetical to *The Axion Esti*, the "Six and One Remorses for the Sky" (1960) was to contrast the longer poem's declarative, solemn, triumphant, often lyrical voice with some few private meditations and whisperings, yet within the same climate. The poet's remorses are for a sky, the transcendent summit of his Eros, which had lost its earlier innocence through the poet's and the world's war and postwar experience. These poems are inner questionings and efforts to pass from a common and personal sense of guilt to a new and liberated awareness, to draw from experience a new knowledge and hope and so help a new sky—now more emphatically an inner one—attain a new purity on a higher and more conscious spiritual level.

In "Beauty and the Illiterate" the poet comes to learn of a feminine beauty of a different kind: the deeper beauty of the suffering soul, a beauty beyond matter, beyond even life itself, the beauty born out of love's tears. The "Autopsy" reveals in the poet's corpse elements and substances testifying to his erotic life and foretelling and promising the fertility of the land: "We shall have early fruit this year." (*SS*, p. 120) Among the things springing from "The Sleep of the Valiant," who sacrificed their lives to the noble cause of life, is "One drop of clear water, hanging courageously over the abyss, they named Arete, and gave her a lean, boyish body." (*SS*, p. 123) "The Other Noah" is the poet himself considering what is to be saved in the Ark of his asceticism "for lust to begin its holy career." Among the things found and saved are *bread, longing, love . . ."* (*SS*, p. 125) As in *The Axion Esti*, an ascent is to follow a downfall, when "the holy day of sensual pleasure may emit its fragrance, / That the Lady, Bearer of Verdure, may ascend naked the stream of Time" accompanied by "The trills of Paradise." (*SS*, p. 126) The "Seven Days for Eternity" are seven short lyrical pieces, considerably erotic and transfigurative, which serve as steps leading again toward a resurrection and paradisiacal blessedness.

Praise of his more recent "Monogram" (1971) pertains primarily to its accomplishment as an art form, the ingenuity of its prosody and its intricate "mathematical" structure. Its thematic content and imagery—where the lonely "I" of the lover addresses softly, affectionately, nostalgically, the ghostly "You" of a lost and recollected beloved now summoned back to enter a paradise to be born within—mark, to some extent, a return to the poet's earlier, idyllic world, enhanced by a craft that has perfectly mastered the simplicity of depth. In its twilight world, the word *agape* (not in the Western theological sense of the term) replaces the word *eros*, and the lover's speech has a hallucinatory quality in addressing a Beatrice-like figure raised to the realm of Ideas. Natural, earthly beauty is still present and is viewed now in the more ethereal light of the beyond.

The pieces in "The Light Tree and the Fourteenth Beauty" (1971) might be called fragments of the new paradise. They are generally lighter, less lonely and less nostalgic in mood than those in "The Monogram." The sky of Palm Sunday brings a young girl who "paused without reason leaving her blouse unbuttoned." In "The Girl the North Wind Brought" the poet is seeking a little chapel as a respite from the wilderness, when the girl appears in a shower of signs and oracles, again Beatrice-like, a recollection "as beautiful as can be," an apparition longed for but elusive and soon to disappear. "Three Times the Truth" presents the poet's search for the "Something else [that] must be found," leading first to the discovery that inner man is "Nobody Nobody!" and soon devolving into a version of the Lord's Prayer:

> *Our Father who art in heaven*   I who have loved   I who have kept my girl like a vow   who could even catch the sun by its wings like a butterfly   *Our Father* I lived on nothing.

(SS, p. 143)

The poet then concludes by stressing again the simplicity of his Paradise: "Until at last I felt and let them call me crazy that out of nothing is born our Paradise." (*SS*, p. 144)

In his "Open Book" (1974) speaking at length about the significance and value of dreams for poetry—a value that surrealism was to take ample advantage of—Elytis recounts some of his own revelatory dreams, and we suspect that some of the poems in "The Light Tree" are essentially dream-poems in nature. In "On the Republic" (another name for his Paradise), for example, the poet builds a Temple out of "four stones and a little sea-water" and sits there waiting. As noon approaches, much as in Mallarmé's "L'après-midi d'un faune," he falls asleep and is visited by a dream (a wet dream) that mixes the four horses of the Apocalypse with a bearded man approaching sexual intercourse with a woman. The dream transforms the world as the poet awakens. In another poem he beckons a thirteen-year-old "Little Green Sea" (the Ionian Sea of his childhood), wanting to sleep "secretly" with her and find in her embrace "Broken stones: the words of God / Broken stones: fragments from Heraklei-tos." (*SS*, p. 146) As for "The Light Tree" poem, that tree (we suspect, a sunray), grown in his backyard, bursts suddenly into blossom through the moisture of his spit, bringing the answer of "truth" to all of his childhood questionings with regard to the meaning of the world and the end of happiness. Evil times have intervened, he finds his beloved island now deserted, and he wonders what has happened to that tree "Now when no one mourns the nightingales and all write poems." (*SS*, pp. 152–53)

In attempting to detect Eros's steps through a bird's-eye view in the expanse of Elytis's verse, we have certainly missed a great deal. We have seen numerous sights shining bright and different, yet springing from the same ground, illumined and nurtured by the same core of light. They are enlivened by a highly active Eros, who has stood at the heart of Elytis's verse from its very beginning. Other themes and forces have been related to that one theme and force, of which they become extensions in the widening of its meaning and creative functions. In terms of origins, Elytis's Eros was already present in the Hesiodic *Theogony* as "that fairest among the deathless gods, who unnerves the limbs and overcomes the mind and wise counsels of all gods and all men within them," but with one significant exception: rather than overcoming, this new Eros has continued composing and creating. Also, according to Sappho (to whom our poet owes much), Eros was the child of Uranus, the Sky; hence his constant longing to rise, with earth, to his father's realm. Elytis's Platonism further expanded the concept and functions of Eros. For Plato's Eros—a daimon rather than a god, by the way—the beauty of the body was to serve as tinder, as bait for the higher aspiration, the beauty of the soul. In Elytis, as we have already remarked, there is a longing for a comparable ascent, a transcendence of matter into spirituality; but for him the two worlds are far from being mutually exclusive. They are together and inseparate, the one an extension of the other and its spiritual completion.

In Plato, there stood behind Eros, leading the soul downward into the depths, the spirit of memory, Mnemosyne, the recollection of an ancient, prenatal happiness in the company of the gods, a eudaimonia we lost when we entered time. The pain of that loss was to spur us toward the recovery of that world of eternal purity. Elytis, too, is full of recollection of a perfect world, not prenatal but earthly, his Aegean, the loss of which causes him his utmost pain; and the effort of his verse is to recover this world imaginatively and to transcend it. Seen in this light, his poetry reflects three gradual stages, the first being that of an innocent, erotic youth in the arms of an Aegean blessedness. The next stage brings the loss of that world and its purity, the loss of youth, the ugly experience of war and the taste of death, where that early world is passionately recollected as a solace. The third stage draws from this experience the elements not only for the recovery of that lost world, but its spiritual justification and transcendence as well. The value of suffering is discovered, together with the heroic and the tragic elements in life. Not only the heavenly heights, but the depths, too, are reached, and all this for the building of a new paradise, as intuitive as the early one, yet also highly conscious. Opposites are reconciled and unified in the light of recollection of that splendid old summer, the realm of the Sun, of Beauty and of Eros, where now Purity and a sun-like Justice are triumphant. This is his paradise within.

"Orientations" and "Sun the First" expressed the first stage. Elytis may later have discredited that early poetry of his from an artistic viewpoint, but we beg to disagree with him to some extent. Some of his loveliest and most cherished poems are in those early collections. The solid foundations of his entire creation are already present. The "Heroic and Elegiac Song" brought in the second stage, that of loneliness, pain and estrangement, with its simultaneous effort to transcend that state through understanding and recollection. The years of silence that followed were also years of meditation and study, as well as years of worldly experience, during which Elytis's intuitive familiarity with his Greekness evolved into a deeper, more intellectual awareness of its ancient, Byzantine and modern tradition and wealth—elements now thoroughly assimilated by his lyrical genius and his prevalent view of life. Time and its tragicality entered his world, and with them came maturity. His symbols gained in breadth and scope. The product was *The Axion Esti*, the core of his work, which in its three parts encompasses all three stages: a "Genesis" to rebuild the universality of the Aegean world, "The Passion" to come to terms with time and experience and set the foundations for a resurrection, and the concluding "Gloria," singing the praise of the resulting new world of Purity and Love, which the "Six and One Remorses" then further refine. As for Elytis's more recent books, they have all centered more or less on his concern for the building of this new inner paradise. Eros had built that first world, in all its innocence, but then vanished for a time in the archetypal, heroic descent into darkness, the archetypal Nekyia. But he remained active even there—in the dark where gold shines, to borrow from Pound—regathering his cosmogonic resources for a new and more powerful rise, a rise full of wisdom.

Odysseus Elytis: A Contemporary Greek Poet

By HANS RUDOLF HILTY

The course of this poet and his fame outside Greece is exemplary in many respects. In 1935—two years after the death of Cavafis—the journal *Nea Ghrámmata* published a first series of his poems; since that time the Greek literary world has counted him among the liveliest voices in the chorus of contemporary poetry. In 1939 the comprehensive collection *Prosanatolizmí* (Orientations) confirmed his rank, and in 1943 there followed the volume *Ílios o prótos* (Sun the First). That same year brought the death of the last great poet of the old generation, Kostis Palamás. Ever since, Elytis has been considered the leading poet of Greece. Outside his homeland, a first sampling of his work appeared in the Swiss journal *Formes et couleurs* (Lausanne), and in the last fifteen years he has become a well-known figure within the learned circles of France, Italy, England and the US. There is scarcely a single prominent literary journal in these countries which has not yet presented a selection of Elytis's poems in translation, his poetry has been included in anthologies, and individual works have been published in book form in French and Italian. Only in the German-speaking realm was there until recently—aside from individual poems which have appeared in the journal *hortulus*—no adaptation.[1] Now, however, the Tschudy-Verlag's "Quadrat-Bücher" series, which publishes Greek texts with German translations on facing pages, has issued a book entitled *Körper des Sommers* (Body of Summer) from one of the poems contained therein. For this volume, a young German archeologist for whom Greece has become a second home, Barbara Schlörb, collaborated with a Greek friend, Antigone Kasoléa, in translating a representative selection of Elytis's work to date, affording the German reader a first glance into the richness of this poet's world.

Elytis (born Odysseás Alepoudhélis) is descended from an old family native to Lesbos and was born in 1911 in Iráklion, Crete—where, by the way, Kazantzakis also first saw the light of day (1883). He grew up in Athens and began studying law in 1930, but soon felt himself drawn more to writing and to art. He was particularly captivated by the expressive world of the French surrealists. He translated Lautréamont, Éluard, Jouve and Lorca into modern Greek, wrote studies on modern art, traveled, then settled for a time in Paris in 1948; and without this expedition into the wide-open spaces, without the element of an open and expanding intellectual curiosity, his poetry would be inconceivable. His roots in the singular nature of his homeland remained strong, however, as was demonstrated during the war, when, following his return from the front, he became a poet of the Greek Resistance through his works "Heroic and Elegiac Song for the Lost Second Lieutenant of the Albanian Campaign"

Hilty's article, which was especially liked and recommended by Elytis himself, originally appeared in the respected Zurich newspaper, the *Neue Zürcher Zeitung*, 17 July 1960; hence the outdated nature of, e.g., the information on German translations of Elytis's poetry, which has been updated in note 1 below.

and the "Albaniad," both of which could only be circulated by hand in manuscript form until the end of the Occupation. Those roots are no less evident in the general mood and tone of all his poems, which evoke the atmosphere of the Aegean landscape with passionate power. The broad perspective of an open mind and a vital, concrete bond with the archetypal gestures of life, magical surrealism and unbroken Hellenic substance merge in this poetry to form painfully illuminating images of Mediterranean existence.

Take, for example, the poem "Body of Summer," which gave the German collection its title:

> A long time has passed since the last rainfall was heard
> Above the ants and the lizards
> Now the sky burns endlessly
> The fruit trees paint their mouths
> The pores of the earth very slowly open
> And beside the trickling and syllabic waters
> A huge plant stares straight into the sun.
>
> Who is this who sprawls on the far beaches
> Stretched on his back, smoking the smokesilver olive leaves
> Crickets warm themselves in his ears
> Ants scurry to work on his chest
> Lizards glide in the long grasses of his armpits
> And through the seaweed of his feet a wave lightly passes
> Sent by that small siren who sang:
>
> "O naked body of summer, burnt
> And eaten away by oil and salt
> Body of rock and the heart's tremor
> Great fluttering in the willow's hair
> Breath of basil on the curly groin
> Filled with starlets and pine needles
> Profound body, vessel of day!"
>
> The slow rains come, the pelting hail,
> The shores pass by, flogged by the claws of the wintry wind
> That with savage billows lowers in the sea-depths
> The hills plunge into thick udders of clouds
> But behind all this you smile unconcernedly
> And find again your deathless hour
> As once more you are found on the beaches by the sun
> And amid your naked vigor by the sky. (pp. 75–76)[2]

The landscape is perceived by the poet as archaically harsh and glaring—considering Elytis's birthplace, one is tempted to say "Cretan"—and man does not appear here as lord of creation, as the measure of all things. Human "Morphé," human form is, to be sure, assumed by the forces of the landscape and of time: the summer, the earth, youth, memory. But man, for his part, is scarcely anything other than a lens, in which the burning force of the landscape and of time is refracted—a reflection, and perhaps a deceptive one. It becomes apparent that whenever Elytis introduces man into the landscape, he almost always resorts to questioning inversions:

> What can you face and what can you wear
> Dressed in the music of grass and how do you proceed
> Amid the sage and the heather . . . (69)

> On your lips there is a taste of storm—But where have
>   you wandered
> All day long with the hard reverie of stone and sea ... (65)

> The age of the sea within your eyes
> And on your body the sun's vigor—what was I looking for
> Deep within sea-caverns amid spacious dreams ... (67)

In the unquestionable process of landscape and time, man is a disruptive, painful question—there is the Act, in which man can participate directly in the unquestion-ableness of nature:

> It was April, I remember, when I felt for the first time
>   your human weight
> Your human body of clay and corruption
> As on our first day on earth
> It was the festival of the amaryllis ... (67)

To be sure, Elytis never speaks of love in the present, but rather always in the form of memory. Memory, however, can incorporate not only things past but also things future; every utterance about paradise lost engenders the hope for a paradise to be regained. "Echo" is both a favorite word and a key word in Elytis's poems. Sky and sea, sea and land, landscape and man, man and woman, and also the ecstasies of time—past, present and future—stand opposite one another in an echo-relationship: the one the echo and reflection of the other. The oeuvre of this Greek poet is a canon of such echoes and reflections. Hence, the singularity of his images: they are never pale, always colorful, vivacious; but as soon as they begin to coalesce into something tangible, they flicker out again. It is in this flickering realm that Elytis finds his most beautiful poetic signatures: "earth of Boeotia brightened by the wind," "dressed in the music of grass," "dust of maiden dreams," "a clover of light on your breast."

In the poetry of Lorca, of Ungaretti, of Quasimodo and of Montale, and in recent Hebrew poetry from Israel, there can be found related poetic emanations of Mediter-ranean life. Precisely such a juxtaposition of thematically similar literary phenomena, however, serves to clarify and delineate the Greek's highly individual poetic profile: it is more expansive and inclusive, with longer lines and multi-layered images. A characteristic feature of the Greek language is that, even in the hands of modern Greek poets, it has preserved a secret affinity to the epic narrative; something of the flow of Homeric verse, something beyond any kind of classicism, is discernible in Cavafis and Elytis.

The most exact parallels to Elytis's poetic images are found, not in the work of other lyric poets, but rather in the essays of Albert Camus. In "Noces" (Nuptials) there are sentences which sound like rational prose paraphrasings of verses by Elytis:

Here, I leave order and moderation to others. The great free love of nature and the sea absorbs me completely. In this marriage of ruins and springtime, the ruins have become stones again, and losing the polish imposed on them by man, they have reverted to nature. To celebrate the return of her prodigal daughters Nature has laid out a pro-fusion of flowers ... How many hours have I spent crushing absinthe leaves, caressing ruins, trying to match my breathing with the world's tumultuous sighs! Deep among wild scents and concerts of somnolent insects, I open my eyes and heart to the unbearable grandeur of this heat-soaked sky. It is not easy to become what one is ...[3]

It would be idle to ask whether Elytis and Camus knew each other or not. What is involved here is by no means anything such as literary "inheritance" or "adaptation," but rather a correspondence between the world experience of two poets of identical age in the midst of the selfsame Mediterranean landscape. For Elytis, the concept "echo" is the key; Camus uses "marriage" in the same sense: "marriage of ruins and springtime," "marriage of light." And where Camus discerns beneath the unbearable vastness of the gleaming sky the summons "to become what one is," Elytis says the following, taken from his poem "Laconic":

> Ardor for death so inflamed me that my radiance returned
>   to the sun,
> And it sends me back into the perfect syntax of stone and
>   air.
> Well then, he whom I sought *I am*. (123)

Here some mention of myth must be made. Ancient Greek history is certainly present on occasion in Elytis's poetry. In the poem "Shape of Boeotia" he asks about the fate of Thebes:

> What has become of the orchestra of nude hands below the
>   palaces
> The mercy that rose like the smoke of holiness
> Where are the gates with archaic birds that sang
> And the clang of metal that daybroke the terror of the people
> When the sun entered like a triumph
> When fate writhed on the lance of the heart
> And the civil strife of birdsong raged
> What has become of the immortal March libations
> Of Greek traceries on the watery grass
>
> Brows and elbows were wounded
> Time from too much sky rolled crimson
> Men advanced
> Laden with lament and dream. (69)

But the poet avoids the names of the Greek myths, and he avoids above all throughout his oeuvre the names of Greek gods and heroes. It would therefore be an unjustified Hellenization if, for example, in the verses just cited, one were to replace "the sun" with "Helios." There is no mythology in Elytis's poetry, but this does not mean that for him there are no gods. Turning to Camus once again, we find on the page following the passage previously quoted, this commentary:

> Those who need myths are indeed poor. Here the gods serve as beds or resting places as the day races across the sky. I describe and say: "This is red, this blue, this green. This is the sea, the mountain, the flowers." Need I mention Dionysus to say that I love to crush mastic bulbs under my nose?

Only in one selection from the volume *Körper des Sommers*, namely, the poem "The Sleep of the Valiant (Variation)," are there classical Greek concepts which have remained untranslated: the three concepts "Hades," "kairos" and "arete." These have proven untranslatable, and it is precisely in this poem—which, like Elytis's magnificent Resistance poems, stems from the theme of Greece's struggle for freedom—that an allusion to the Greek national spirit seems justified. In the poem, arete takes on human form:

> One drop of clear water, hanging courageously over the abyss,
>   they named Arete, and gave her a lean, boyish body.
>
> All day now young Arete descends and labors hard in those
>   places where the earth was rotting out of ignorance, and
>   where men inexplicably had committed their dark iniquities. (123)

This Arete is no classical goddess of valor in the heroic mold, but rather a little girl with a slender, boyish body who labors the whole day through at what has been neglected. Similarly, Jean Anouilh's Antigone in the play of the same name is no heroine of tragic grandeur, but instead a stubborn young girl, "the skinny little thing sitting back over there and saying nothing"; but she alone will defy Creon. The parallel is exact. Anouilh's Antigone is to Sophocles's heroine as Elytis's Arete is to the Arete or Virtus of classical antiquity.

The fact that this transformation has taken place in the work of a Greek poet, writing in Greek and on Greek soil, in precisely the same fashion as in the work of a French playwright is interesting enough. In regard to Elytis's entire accomplishment, the image of this "little Arete" attests anew to the fact that Hellenic substance lives on in modern Greek literature with a vitality which increases in direct proportion to the decisive subjugation of classicism. In the process of this transformation, the regenerative power of life becomes apparent in the transformation of language and in the transformation of human ideals—and in the capacity for creative communication. Understood in these terms, Odysseus Elytis can rightfully be considered the most representative poet of present-day Greece. And understood in these terms, the oft-repeated twaddle contrasting "tradition and modernity" collapses as soon as we come upon a genuine work of art.

Translated from the German
By
William Riggan

---

[1] Several translations of Elytis's work have appeared since the writing of this article: a number of his poems are included in Otto Staininger's *Griechische Lyrik der Gegenwart*, Linz, Wimmer, 1960; seven nocturnes have been translated by Günter Dietz as *Sieben nächtliche Siebenzeiler*, Darmstadt, Bläschke, 1966; and Dietz has also published *To Áxion Estí—Gepriesen Sei*, Hamburg, Claassen, 1969.

[2] Page numbers refer to Elytis's *The Sovereign Sun*, Kimon Friar, tr., Philadelphia, Temple University Press, 1974.

[3] Albert Camus, *Lyrical and Critical Essays*, Philip Thody, ed., Ellen Conroy Kennedy, tr., New York, Knopf, 1969, pp. 66–67.

Elytis and French Poetry 1935-1945

By CHRISTOPHER ROBINSON

The fascination that French poetry exerted on Elytis is a force in his creative development to which he himself has frequently referred, but only in general terms. It has been described as the influence of "surrealism," but that in itself is an umbrella concept covering a great many different writers and approaches to poetry. To define the French influence we must look first at what overlap exists between the esthetic views of Elytis and those of his French contemporaries, and then see how far that common view of poetry is the controlling factor in Elytis's own poetic development.

For an insight into his early esthetic views, some of the best evidence is contained in two articles published in the periodical *Nea Ghrámmata* in 1944. The first, written two years previously and looking back to the start of the poet's career in the mid–1930s, forms a detailed poetic credo: the second reinterprets certain esthetic issues in response to an attack by the writer and critic Constantine Tsatsos. Elytis here explores the problems of function and form interdependently. He is a universalist and anti-materialist, calling for the "initiation of man, body and soul, into the essence of things, into the secret of their identification with the essence of the Universe," an initiation which poetry can achieve by appealing to the totality of man, and especially to emotive and intuitive man, in such a way that he achieves an instinctive spiritual identity with material creation. It is this need to sensitize untapped areas of human experience that imposes the need for new form, for if poetry is to be exploratory, language must also be so; it cannot acknowledge conventions of either esthetics or logic. In all this Elytis follows the more modest proposals of contemporary French theorists, with due acknowledgment to Breton's *Les vases communicants* (1934) and Éluard's *Donner à voir* (1932). But none of the seven central principles of modernism that are offered would have been unacceptable to Laforgue or Rimbaud.[1] When Tsatsos challenged him on the conservatism of his position, Elytis concentrated his defense on a specific but equally conservative area of ideas, propounding a view of the poet and of poetic communication that is positively Baudelairean. The poet is an interpreter: "If there is a quality with which the poet is endowed that makes him stand out from other men, . . . it is precisely the possession of the capacity to grasp by supraintellectual means, i.e., in an immediately poetic fashion, the conjunctions of moments in his own soul and in the soul of the material world around him, which are fleeting and difficult to grasp." More interestingly still, he extended his defense (against automatic writing) of the poet's right to "select" into a reinstatement of intellect in poetry,[2] defining its role as that force which constrains a poem to present in its totality a completed image, itself constituting an idea and composed out of independent smaller images.

In fact, what Elytis means when he aligns himself with the French surrealists is simply a) that he accepts the attempt to achieve an ideal world without giving up the values of the sensual world, and b) that he accepts the role of poetry as a revelatory medium rather than a literary form. He himself seems to realize that, in that sense, his use of the term "surrealist" is misleading, for he concludes his reply to Tsatsos by maintaining that it is merely a convenient label for a group of experimenters who are not held by it to fixed beliefs on any aspect of poetry, since their allegiance is to the ideal of poetry itself and not to a school. Clearly Elytis's views sit awkwardly along-side the official surrealist line proposed by Breton.[3] If his attachments to modernity in French poetry lie anywhere, it is not there, but rather in the work of individual poets. The obvious choices are two poets, the second not a surrealist at all, whom he mentions in the first of the *Nea Ghrámmata* articles: ". . . two contemporary French poets, not among the most famous, Paul Éluard and Pierre Jean Jouve, compelled me to become aware of, and unhesitatingly accept, the possibilities which lyric poetry offered when practiced in a spirit of freedom."

Again we have a direct insight into Elytis's interpretation of both poets; for in *Nea Ghrámmata* for 1936 he published a short article on Éluard with a number of translations of his poems, and a similar article on Jouve, also accompanied by a set of translations, appeared in the same periodical in 1938. The interest lies less in the articles themselves, which are brief introductions to the major aspects of the two poets, than in the choice of poems for translation, which represents a more personalized view on Elytis's part of where their poetic interest lies. In the discussion of Éluard, Elytis concentrates largely on compositional aspects, stressing that the elliptic syntax, reliance on conglomerations of logically unrelated images and the boldness of epithets all con-tribute to the immediacy of poetic communication by eliminating rational response. He mentions the degree to which Éluard, in practicing Rimbaud's "dérèglement de tous les sens," creates a new relationship between the inner self and the outer world, but this aspect of the poems is subordinated to a discussion of their impact as groups of images. In all this Elytis emphasizes the "surreal" elements of disconnectedness and "surprise." But when we turn to the poems chosen, the impression is rather different. Rather than the Éluard of "la terre est bleu comme une orange,"[4] Elytis has selected eleven poems that represent Éluard in his more direct approach to the physical world and the human senses, where the interpenetration of man and nature in erotic imagery is more easily accessible to the reader.

I am not suggesting that Elytis in any way misrepresents Éluard. His selection emphasizes the way in which Éluard's poems appeal to the senses in their imagery, with nature, especially sunlight, birds and stones, and the four elements very much to the fore, alongside the human body. But it also shows the degree to which Éluard's images are not random, that, as Bachelard put it, "Les images germent bien, elles poussent bien, elles poussent droit. Chez Éluard les images ont raison." The following poem, the second of Elytis's translations, is a good example of this.[5]

> Plume d'eau claire pluie fragile
> Fraîcheur voilée de caresses
> De regards et de paroles
> Amour qui voile ce que j'aime.

The association of love with a dynamic universal element, water, and the underlying paradox of clarity that obscures (rain veiling nature, love veiling the beloved) are controlling features of the poem, giving a very definite shape to its overall idea. In that sense the poem precisely fulfills Elytis's canon of how intellect may play a role in poetic creation. The composite picture of Éluard's poems offered by Elytis's selection is primarily that of this interrelation between psychological states—mostly erotic—and the external world through carefully selected sets of images blending dynamic and static qualities in a language that is highly elliptic but firmly grounded in the vocabulary of ordinary life. That is a somewhat different picture from the one offered by the article.

We can observe a similar pattern in Elytis's translations from Jouve. This time, the article concerns itself less with technical matters than with the metaphysical implications of Jouve's poetry, which Elytis defines as blending mysticism, awareness of death, erotic passion, the forces of nature and the desire for a permanent solution to the paradox of life. He describes the development of thought between *Les noces* (1931) and *Matière céleste* (1937), as Jouve found himself increasingly obliged to acknowledge that material perceptions cannot be dissociated from spiritual ones, and concludes that this is the poetry of a tragic and tormented idealist. Emphasis is naturally placed on the importance of the subconscious for Jouve as that part of the individual containing dark forces common to all men, and on the esthetic implication of this for the role of the image; but there is no attempt to accommodate Jouve to a surrealist view of poetic communication. Indeed, why should there be, when Jouve had already formulated, in the preface to *Sueur de sang* (1933), the tenet which Elytis was to propose in 1944 as the core of his "surrealist" approach: "Dans son expérience actuelle, la poésie est en présence de multiples condensations à travers quoi elle arrive à toucher au symbole—non plus contrôlé par l'intellect, mais surgi, redoutable et réel"? The only slight distortion in his theoretical presentation of Jouve—but it will be a significant one—is the insistence on the importance of the physical world, for, though important to the thought of the poetry, it plays a lesser part in the imagery than is suggested.

However, the selection of poems by Jouve that Elytis translates is a great deal less representative than the objectivity of his article might lead one to expect. *Les noces* as a collection expresses a tension between a sense of guilt and horror inspired by the material world and a vision of ecstasy contained in fragmented glimpses of man's spiritual goal. Physical desire, which recurs as a leitmotif of disgust, is not simply a human function, but an aspect under which the whole of material creation is to be condemned:

> Les collines ont d'affreuses douceurs
> Le passant y mesure ses anciens péchés.
> Qui peut apprécier leur végétation
> Et résister au mouvement lascif de ces hanches?[6]

Elytis, however, concentrates on the transcendental aspect, completely unbalancing the tension. Only one of his poems, "La mélancolie d'une belle journée," represents hostility to unregenerated nature, whereas eight offer the perception of the calm, still world of the Ideal in which the physical world is portrayed in a purified form: "Les arbres quand on les mesure sont bleus de joie."[7] He has a particular penchant for the section "Jardin des âmes au printemps," with its images of refuge, purity and elevation:

> L'oiseau translucide au-dessus du temple
> Annonce et s'évase, oh son cri profond:
> Quiconque m'aime m'écoute.[8]

This emphasis on the achievement of reconciliation between flesh and spirit is completed by the inclusion of "Vrai corps," the single poem which forms the concluding section of the collection and in which Jouve uses the Crucifixion as an image of reconciliation without convincing the reader that the validity of the image is much more than esthetic.

There is no sense of inevitable evolution toward achievement in *Les noces*, yet Elytis has contrived to give it such an orientation by selecting predominantly triumphant poetry in which the material world has been in some way regenerated. Understandably, he has, then, taken a much smaller selection from *Sueur de sang*; for though in that collection Jouve begins to face the problem of incorporating the material world into the redemptive process, there is no acceptance of matter as such—indeed, the poet feels a sense of exhaustion before the full spectacle of human horror. Elytis contents himself with selecting poems that overlap with the main lines (as he presents them) of *Les noces* and *Matière céleste*. In this last collection, virtually ignoring the poems of the "Nada" section and the blacker aspects of the theme "Le désir de la chair est désir de la mort," he concentrates on the Hélène sequence, where sensual and spiritual are at last fully synthesized. The central image is of the woman who, in dying, has fulfilled her greatest potential and become a living symbol infusing spiritual force into the landscape. Through her the hero gains both the physical fulfillment of consummated love and the spiritual illumination necessary to his transcendence of the material. The final image for both Jouve and Elytis is thus that of Orpheus, who undergoes the consummation, loss and transfiguration, but who also symbolizes the poet in his role as interpreter of this ultimate experience.

What emerges from this study of Elytis's choice of texts for translation is an unexpected overlap between the poetic worlds of Éluard and Jouve, an overlap which suggests that the Greek poet has made his selection not on a basis of chance, or because these particular poems were easier to translate, and certainly not because they were representative in a conventional sense. He seems to have chosen the poems because he felt a particular affinity with their form and the emotive interpretation of the world that they offer. Éluard has, of course, no overt transcendental side, but his eroticism is projected outward to effect a fusion between universal forces and inner feelings. Jouve is brought closer to him by the emphasis on his fascination with the physical world and with what he once called "la pauvre, la belle puissance érotique humaine." At the same time, the more violently surreal aspects of Éluard's technique are passed over, so that, in terms of poetic control, there is a more apparent connection between his style and the poems of *Les noces*, at least. Both poets are presented by Elytis as appealing emotively, through sets of related if elliptic images drawn from nature, to the subconscious responses in man, which will give him a new and largely joyous vision of his integration into the world about him.

Can we detect a significant relationship between those aspects of the two French poets to which Elytis seems to have been drawn and the development of his own poetry in the period 1935–45? It is hardly possible with this type of poetry to talk of influences in a conventional sense, that is, of common themes and images. We can look, however, for common attitudes to life and to the problems of poetic communication raised by those attitudes. "Orientations" (1939) contains all the poems that

Elytis thought worth preserving from what he had written up to that date, and it is, accordingly, a very disparate collection. But many of the poems are built up from a series of images interrelating man and his environment, emotion and action, individual and universal in just such a way as we have seen them used by Éluard.

> Summer's labors turn golden,
> The just hypostasis of the sun. See the faces
> Ashen and bare
> Burned inwardly.
>
> And the plain undulates Love
> Undulates the secret world
>
> Pure hymn of life.

The activity of the physical world is seen in strong visual images (gold and blood for sun and the maturation of the summer landscape), but images which, like Éluard's, carry a human dimension (toil) and a dynamic movement (the undulation of the plain). Man is affected in both his bodily sensations and his emotions by the same elemental force (Eros), whose outward agent is the sun and which is also contained in the images of fire and water that are associated with it. Like Éluard's poems, too, is the elliptic syntax and the intellectual organization of the images into a compact group, which is nonetheless accessible only via a direct emotional response. The poem is typical of the sequence in which it stands and has common qualities with the series of prose poems "The Concert of Hyacinths"; but the later poems of "Orientations," while employing the same elements, reveal a more conventional thematic framework, in which the problems of time, memory, pain and doubt accompany the more hallucinatory evocations of erotic forces in the universe:

> With sand on my fingers, I would close my fingers
> With sand in my eyes, I would clench my fingers
> This was torment—
> It was April, I remember, when I felt for the first
>   time your human weight
> Your human body of clay and corruption.[9]

If there are influences here, they are surely of Seferis rather than of the French.

Nonetheless, the cycle "Sun the First" (1943) confirms the predominance, at this stage of Elytis's development, of the ecstatic celebration of the natural world under its positive aspect. The poems are under the "sign" of the sun, consciously rejecting the significance of death: "I know the night no longer, the terrible anonymity of death." Let us take a typical stanza from "Body Summer":

> "O naked body of summer, burnt
> And eaten away by oil and salt
> Body of rock and the heart's tremor
> Great fluttering in the willow's hair
> Breath of basil on the curly groin
> Filled with starlets and pine needles
> Profound body, vessel of day!"[10]

Elytis here makes central Éluard's blending of the human body and the natural world, such that the two offer a single response to the light, heat and luxuriance of summer. Man and his environment are no longer divisible, either physically or in the spiritual pursuit of their journey, whose mysteries are only hinted at in the image of the stars.

The images retain Éluard's interest in the visual and the dynamic; yet the restraining role of intellect is much more plainly felt than before. Elsewhere in the collection this same restraining intellect surfaces as a direct poetic voice, conscious of its isolated creative purpose in a hostile environment:

> With what stones, what blood, and what iron,
> With what fire are we made
> Though we seem pure mist
> And they stone us and say
> That we walk with our heads in the clouds.[11]

Again Elytis has moved away from his French mentors into new paths.

Éluard's influence seems, then, to have been important to Elytis's initial formulation of his own relationship with the physical world around him and to his search for a poetic expression appropriate to that relationship.[12] In the sense that the Jouve who is presented through Elytis's translations is so close in his ecstatic vision of nature, we should probably attribute the elements already discussed as much to his influence as to Éluard's. But can we detect a separate influence of Jouve? The answer would seem to be negative for the poems of this period. What would perhaps merit study is the separate issue of whether the new metaphysical dimension which marks Elytis's later poems, "Six and One Remorses for the Sky" and *The Axion Esti*, both of which appeared after some fifteen years of poetic silence, has any relation to Jouve's transcendental synthesis of flesh and spirit. The "Gloria" section of *The Axion Esti*, with its transfiguration of the beauty of the physical world into an expression of eternal abstracts, has certain superficial elements in common with the same theme in *Matière céleste*, and perhaps also with Jouve's *Kyrie* (1938), in which he maintains a complete unity of thought, imagination and sensual perception within an explicitly Christian framework. If the metaphysical aspect of Jouve seriously influenced Elytis, this has not appeared in his writing until these later works. And yet, the final lines of the *Kyrie* would make a fitting epitaph to any phase of Elytis's poetry: "Tout est profond tout est sans faute et cristallin / Tout est vert bleu tout est joyeux est azurin."

---

[1] For example: "A significant area of life cannot be expressed within the realm of the conscious."

[2] This is incorporated into a footnote. Perhaps Elytis felt the point too controversial for the body of the text.

[3] Even Breton had momentary doubts about automatic writing. But he never swerved from the hostility toward the intellect which marks the 1924 *Manifeste*: "Le surréalisme repose sur la croyance à la réalité supérieure de certaines formes d'association négligées jusqu'à lui, à la toute-puissance du rêve, au jeu désintéressé de la pensée. Il tend à ruiner définitivement tous les autres mécanismes psychiques."

[4] *L'amour, la poésie*, section VII, in *Paul Éluard: Oeuvres complètes*, Paris, Pléiade, vol. 1, p. 232. All references will be given according to this edition.

[5] The poems translated by Elytis are given, for convenience, in the original French. This poem is "L'univers solitaire VII," ibid., p. 293.

[6] All references to Jouve will be given according to the Mercure de France edition of the *Poésie*. This poem is "Jaune," vol. 1, p. 32.

[7] "L'esprit jeune," ibid., p. 69.

[8] "Glorieux âge," ibid., p. 70.

[9] Odysseus Elytis, "Sun the First," in *The Sovereign Sun*, Kimon Friar, tr., Philadelphia, Temple University Press, 1974, p. 67.

[10] Ibid, p. 75.

[11] *Six Poets of Modern Greece*, Edmund Keeley and Philip Sherrard, trs., New York, Knopf, 1961, p. 159.

[12] I refer, of course, only to potential influence in the period 1935–45. The problem of the relationship between the two poets in the postwar period is a separate and complex one.

Aspects of Surrealism in the Works of Odysseus Elytis

By ROBERT JOUANNY

It is generally recognized that Elytis, as well as Gátsos, Engonópoulos, Embirícos and several others, gives proof of the existence and influence of surrealism in contemporary Greek poetry. Without reexamining this statement—which, like all literary assimilation, can only be an approximation—it would be interesting to see what has happened today to that supposed surrealist inspiration and to observe the evolution of the poet since his recent work *Ta ro tou érota* (The Ro of Eros; Athens, Asterías, 1972), containing forty-five songs, the earliest of which are fifteen years old.

"A book of songs?" one might ask, as though to disparage it and reject it as evidence. That would be forgetting that today, and more precisely since surrealist poetry has become widespread, songs are more closely associated with poetry, in a sort of spontaneous flow of images and rhythms. We know, too, the interest that people like Desnos and Éluard had in that form of expression which is the least voluntary of all, the counting-rhyme or *comptine*, which is neither song nor poetry and yet is already song and poetry from its very inception. What fortunate encounters there have been in the last quarter of a century between Éluard, Aragon, Prévert, the musicians and the most important contemporary French singers. All the more reason to admit that a Greek poet of today can express himself as perfectly through song as through more ambitious poetry; the collaboration of Elytis and Theodhorákis, which has contributed so greatly to the public's knowledge of *The Axion Esti*, shows to what extent Greek poetry remains, as its tradition demands, a *carmen*, which implies etymologically the resorting to song. That, too, is the case of the songs of "The Ro of Eros," almost half of which have been effectively set to music by Theodhorákis, Birbílis, Kókotos and Hadzidhákis and sung by Dora Yannakópoulos, Gr. Bithikótsis and Maria Pharandoúri, among others. Last of all it should be noted—and this is not the least important justification—that Elytis, in his preface, reserves a choice place for songs alongside his poems.

> Along with my poems, I have also tried to write some songs, for which I have no less respect. In one way or another, one speaks of the same things, the things that one loves, and from there on, it is up to the listeners to judge. It is said that the genre has certain rules of its own. I do not know them, and in any case, I either did not care for or perhaps could not follow them. Each man works according to the way he feels.[1]

The reason is understood, and the distinction between poetry and song poses a false problem, especially with a poet like Elytis.

*

The terms "song" and "spontaneous poetry" should not mislead us: Elytis's book is rich in "literary" resonances, surrealistic or simply contemporary. Proof of this is found in the fact that he proposes the translation of four of Brecht's songs from *The Caucasian Chalk Circle* and of "twelve songs by Lorca"—although the author does not say so precisely, the latter are all inspired by (rather than translated from) García Lorca's *Romancero gitano* (1928). We know how much influence the Andalusian had on the postwar Greeks. Elytis's interest in the *Romancero* comes perhaps closer to being a fad than a deep liking. Besides, it is important to remember that his "translations" were made (he admits it someplace) not from the original text but from what was surely a French translation. This intervention of an intermediary is explanation enough for the liberties Elytis takes with the text, which he "Hellenizes" to the point of suggesting a truly original creation. He neglects, moreover, to translate the six poems that are the most typically and historically Spanish, thus showing that he likes García Lorca more for his qualities as a poet than as an expounder of Spanish realities.[2]

More significant, however, than these admitted borrowings are the similarities of form and the thematic harmonies that give particular proof of a perfect knowledge of Éluard's poetry. Similarities of form, first of all, sometimes limited to a verse, to an image, need only a single example to become evident: the movement and certain images of the poem "Sou to pa yia ta sínefa" (I Told It to You for the Clouds) are in perfect harmony with Éluard's poem *L'amour, la poésie* (1929):

> Je te l'ai dit pour les nuages
> Je te l'ai dit pour l'arbre de la mer
> Pour chaque vague pour les oiseaux dans les feuilles
> Pour les cailloux du bruit
> Pour les mains familières
> Pour l'oeil qui devient visage ou paysage
> Et le sommeil lui rend le ciel de sa couleur
> Pour toute la nuit bue
> Pour la grille des routes
> Pour la fenêtre ouverte pour un front découvert
> Je te l'ai dit pour tes pensées pour tes paroles
> Toute caresse toute confiance se survivent.

It is true that Elytis's poem is more ample, its imagination more diverse, its confidence perhaps more discreet than Éluard's; but it would be easy to demonstrate that whatever is not a direct echo of "Je te l'ai dit . . ." is nonetheless in harmony with all of Éluard's lyricism of love. It is enough to cite three of the Greek poet's stanzas:

> I told it to you for the clouds, I told it to you for your tearful eyes, for the marks left by your hands on the little wet tables, in broad daylight and in secret, I told it to you for the clouds, for you and for me.
>
> I told it to you with the waves, I told it to you with dark whirlwind with the dog and with the dark lantern with the coffee and with the fortune-teller in a whisper and out loud, I told it to you with the waves, I told it to you in the night.
>
> I told it to you at midnight I told it to you when you were not speaking, when I hardly touched you a little with my thought, when the dress you were wearing was in flames, near and afar, I told it to you at midnight with the stars you were looking at.

The themes treated in "The Ro of Eros," when one takes into consideration the more familiar nature of song and of all Greek poetry, are often in harmony with Éluardian themes. Without claiming that one can find behind these graceful and brisk verses all of Elytis's moral and sentimental problematic questions, one can still discover several guiding ideas/images underlying a naïvely narrative plot.

The constant preoccupation of the poet is to reach unremitting familiarity with a world of harmony in which elementary categories and everyday taboos would be forgotten. To become the bridegroom of the sky ("I máyia" [The Maya]), to see boats sail up to balconies and hydrangias fly like swallows ("Ta dhate ta máthate" [Have You Seen and Have You Learned]), to see stones become larger and branches grow ("I panayía tou kimitiríon [Our Lady of the Cemeteries]), to cut out letters in the sun ("O haméleon" [The Chameleon]), are dreams of every poet who, ignoring the limits of the real world, wants to reach a surreal world where all conciliation is conceivable, a world in which—a constant theme of Éluard's poetry—earth, air and sea are harmoniously associated: "Between Syros and Dzia / there grows a bitter-orange tree / my lovely little girl / At the bottom of the sea grow its roots / its branches reach the sky / the little girl I love." (p. 23)

How can one obtain "the golden key with which the heavens are opened" ("To hriso klidhi")? The poet of "the deserted island" is slightly tempted by solitude: "In the wind of wilderness / all is suddenly sanctified / you touch the hand of God / repose upon the waves / like a wild pigeon." (28) But solitude or an indifferent rapport with others is ineffective; there is a lack of communication with beings and with the world: "In our world alas / the algae have no smell / the pebbles do not shine / There are a thousand ambushers / that silently look at you." (47)

Woman alone can establish this relationship; and here, too, Elytis follows in the footsteps of a Breton or an Éluard. With unhappy love the world disappears: "My eyes see lands vanishing / and the world diminishing." (19) With happy love, the world takes on new meaning: "When a love is born / no man can wear it out / and Hades is defeated." (18) Indeed, the reality of love is associated with this major theme of surrealism, the metamorphosis of the world through the intermediacy of omnipotent woman, who alone is capable of passing from a caress to the affirmation of her power: "In the darkness of the garden / you shine only through your caress / But when you enter the house / you eclipse the Evening Star." (63) She alone can give "the powerful light to the Sun and to Death" (44); she alone has "the sun for clothes and the waves for her footsteps" (23); she alone can transform a transparent stone into a tear (37), while, left to himself, the poet, in vain, leaves his heart in the sand like a shell which no one will find. (39) The image of a completely complementary couple comes to him: "I have made of you my shirt / I wear you as I walk / With half of my body / in yours which I hold."[3] (57)

Once this association of two beings is realized, the attainment of a world of harmony is assured. (Is this perhaps the role of the alphabet of Love proposed by "The Ro of Eros"? Familiarity with the elements, with nature, with beings, is gained to such a degree that the role of the poet himself becomes secondary, as the last quatrain of "The Ro of Eros" indicates: "O, had I an eraser / that could efface what is written / I would erase the quatrains / and so keep only you." (63) The song of love, like the song of the "girls of Ispahan," finally leads to a lesson of serenity, of joyful abandon, perhaps even of renunciation: "To sleep to sleep you go / you will find God everywhere / in the bed and in the tomb." (51)

These few rapid notations on Elytis's themes point out sufficiently all the seriousness that goes into the apparent futility of these songs and place this little book in the perspective of surrealist questioning of the relationships between man and the world, of the true reality of the world and of the mediation of the love relationship. Further-more, in order to evoke all the surrealist aspects of this poetry, it would be necessary to stress the role of the images, which are perhaps freer here than in any other book by this poet, because of the spontaneous and lively nature inherent in songs. These images of different origins, borrowed from Greek nature, from the animal or mineral world, follow each other without the slightest concern for logical discourse, as the scent of jasmine evokes the rustling of an angel's wing, sour-orange trees walk like girls and greyhounds leap to catch marigolds on the ceiling—oneiric visions in which the chain of dreams appears to be the arbitrary Ariadne's thread of surreal knowledge: "Rinse us with dream / with the water of carnations / so that we can fill our sorrow / with all that we lack."

This strong visual aspect of Elytis's poetry is confirmed, moreover, by the presence here of nine "collages," done in a surrealist manner by the poet between 1966 and 1972. We know of Elytis's friendship with the collector and critic Tériade, we know the role he played in the "discovery" of the painter Theófilos, and it might be useful to recall that in 1973 he published a book on Theófilos. In it we find that he is sensitive to the ability of "making one see," which poets envy in painters, and that he is con-vinced that a pure heart will always permit the supernatural to reveal itself. He tries to evoke this supernatural, so foreign to the logic of words, through the irrationality of verbal images and, in "The Ro of Eros," through rhythm and the playing with sounds; but he also has the feeling that the visual image will contribute to its retention and to its perceptibility. This role played by his "collages" can be compared to the "repetitions" which in 1922 brought Éluard and Max Ernst close together; these are different expressions of the same problems.

The "collages" presented by Elytis are of interest because they are the work of the poet and give proof of a permanence of visual themes, beyond language, rather than of a fortuitous encounter. Each of nine "collages" deserves to be commented on, even if their artistic quality is unequal, because they permit us to catch a glimpse of the poet's imagination: "The Garden Looks," "Nocturnal Song," "Angel of Astypalea," "Bottom of the Sea," "Ecstasy," "The Woman with the Hand," "Little Love," "Mask" and "Inverted Landscape." These have three dominant themes: 1) the theme of the mirror and the related ones of the look and the inverted landscape; 2) the super-natural, represented by angels, a Cupid, a bronze statue with living eyes, disturbing masks; and 3) familiarity with the real, proceeding from a profusion of roses to the barren sight of the Greek countryside. Playing on the ambiguity of the real world, they sometimes have no connection with the subject of the poem they are supposed to "illustrate," and sometimes they are connected to it by a detail, a fleeting reference to its narrative thread. In any case, they play upon the real/unreal duality and can be "read" either as disturbing questions about the world or as comforting affirmations. Even when they concern the nakedness of a woman in a mirror, a cat standing in front of a candle, a hand in a white glove, the strange is part of the real; this is even more the case when Greece is present.

Elytis's originality in the surrealist stream is based on a sureness that he shares with most Greek poets. If European surrealism is the search for an indeterminate "something else"—"I prefer to walk in the night believing that I am someone who is walking in the day," Breton says in *Nadja*—Elytis finds sureness in the image of Greece. He states that, during their first interview, in 1946, Éluard evoked with emotion the fervor of the first years of surrealism: "Everything was possible then." For Elytis, it is as though this "possible" has become embodied in the reality/surreality of Greece. A country of myths where it is normal to find the supernatural on every shore, Greece, as far as myth is concerned, plays more or less the role that Paris, its streets and its daily life played for French surrealists. But instead of being an arbitrary mental construct depending upon a certain point of view, multidimensional Greek reality—poetic, sensual, intoxicating, legendary, commonplace, made of flowers, perfumes, place-names, insects, angels and sunshine—foists itself, in the twisting of each poem, upon Brecht and Lorca (lemonade becomes raki, p. 80) like the present and elusive idea which is fundamental to poetry itself. The "collages" confirm this real/ surreal ambivalence of Greece, since at least five of them—not to mention the ecstatic cat standing in front of the candle or the multicolored fish—join the supernatural (bronze statue, angels, Cupid) with a photographic representation (undoubtedly fragments of postcards) of the Greek mainland and islands. This is a realistic representation whose realism, in two cases, is denied (or more strongly affirmed?) by an inversion of images in an attempt to show that notions of above and below, of front and reverse cannot be maintained in the face of such abundance. Is that the secret and the raison d'être of these collages? In any case they confirm the role of Greece in Elytis's poetry; and once again it is perhaps the association, aside from all "regionalism," of a known and recognizable land (Astypalea, for example) with a certain mystery that constitutes Elytis's original and authentic contribution to surrealist poetry, an originality whose magic appeal had already been felt through the simple enumeration of the names of women and islands in *The Axion Esti*.

Translated from the French
By
Seymour Feiler

[1] Translations from "The Ro of Eros" have been provided by Andonis Decavalles of Fairleigh Dickinson University.

[2] The neglected poems are: "San Miguel," "San Rafael," "San Gabriel," "Romance de la Guardia Civil española" and the "tres romances históricos." Original titles cannot always be recognized from Elytis's titles. We should point out that "Romance de la luna, luna" corresponds to poem 11, "I selíni sto sidherádhiko" (The Moon in the Forge); "Preciosa y el aire" to poem 1, "Tou anémou ke tis peneménis" (Of the Wind and the Virtuous Maid); "Reyerta" to poem 10, "Ta makhéria" (The Knives); "Romance sonambulo" to poem 12, "Ipnovatiko traghoúdhi" (Song of the Sleepwalker); "La monja gitana" to poem 2, "I kalóghriai téngana" (The Gypsy Nun); "La casada infiel" to poem 9, "I mikropantreméni" (The One Married Young); "Romance de la pena negra" to poem 3, "I kura i pantermi" (The Desolate Lady); "Prendimiento de Antoñito el Camborio en el camino de Sevilla" to poem 6, "O António Tórres Kherédia sto frómo tis Sevíllias" (Antonio Torres Heredia on the Way to Seville); "Muerte de Antonio el Camborio" to poem 7, "Thánatos tou António Tórres Kherédia" (The Death of Antonio Torres Heredia); "Muerto de amor" to poem 4, "Hamos amo agápi" (Dead from Love); and "Romance del emplazado" to poem 5, "Tou pikraménou" (The Embittered One). It can be seen that even the order of the poems has been rearranged for no apparent reason.

[3] The same image is found in Éluard's "Ta foi": "Suis-je autre chose que ta force? / Ta force dans tes bras, / Ta tête dans tes bras, / Ta force dans le ciel décomposé, / Ta tête lamentable, / Ta tête que je porte. / Tu ne joueras plus avec moi, / Heroïne perdue, / Ma force bouge dans tes bras." (From *Capitale de la doleur*)

The "Heroic and Elegiac Song for the Lost Second Lieutenant of the Albanian Campaign": The Transition from the Early to the Later Elytis

By VINCENZO ROTOLO

The poetry of Odysseus Elytis prior to the *Ázma iroikó ke pénthimo yia ton haméno anthipolohaghó tis Alvanías* (Heroic and Elegiac Song for the Lost Second Lieutenant of the Albanian Campaign) has long engaged the critics' attention. In addition to those who stubbornly rejected all innovation, even Marxist criticism, which in Greece more than anywhere was rooted in the then current concept of socialist realism, was unkindly disposed toward Elytis's first compositions. He was even stigmatized as a "Sunday" poet. Though the supporters of modern poetry had accepted the technical novelties of his language, they had stereotyped him as an aristocratic, solitary poet who could only sing lyrically of the beauty of nature and life. This conventional frame managed to stand even after *Ílios o prótos* (Sun the First; 1943), but with the "Heroic Song" (1945) it completely broke down. Those critics who had sustained him felt they had been betrayed (many years later they were to complain of a yet more clamorous "betrayal" in *The Axion Esti*), and they reproached him for deserting his world of blissful youth. But here a preliminary remark should be made.

Elytis's early poetical works, later collected in *Prosanatolizmí* (Orientations; 1939), have certain definite features that reappear in the already-mentioned "Sun the First." As regards technique, the main innovation is in the use of language, which constitutes one of the most personal and most successful adaptations in European poetry of the dictates of "automatic writing," with linguistic and structural implications going far beyond a well-learned lesson. In Elytis, an extraordinary linguistic sensibility succeeds in reconciling the absolute freedom of lexical and semantic transcription of the world of the unconscious with the discipline of a man who shows meticulous care for the language he uses. As regards content, the most prominent feature is the vast range of sensations and notations with which the poet expresses his relationship with the outside world and with his own self. The contemplation of the natural beauty of Greece and of the Aegean in particular, a point on which critics have dwelled considerably, is indeed an expression of a state of ecstasy, of exultation with life; but it also conceals a heartfelt need to seek to commune with nature because of the impossibility of communicating with "the others." Man, in Elytis's poetry, is either absent or no more than an indistinct, shadowy figure. Even in his early phase, the poet knows full well the notes of gloom, the heavy presence of darkness, even though he strives to counter them with light, with the sun.[1] Elytis's youthful attitude is therefore due to his own personal difficulty of finding human contacts rather than to any real desire to avoid them. (At most, one might speak of a certain political disengagement, then quite common, in a period when extremely few intellectuals denounced, for example, the dramatic situation of victims of political persecution struggling for better social justice.)

With the war between Italy and Greece, the poet comes to maturity. This war not only snatches him away from his solitary life, thrusting him into a wider human context; it also enables him to acquire a political conscience by showing him that the rights of the weak are being trampled underfoot by the strong and powerful. The "Heroic Song" is therefore not so much a turning point as a continuation of what the poet has already set out to do. There is also another much stronger thread connecting the early Elytis to the later poet—Greece. The Greece for which he had always felt the most soul-stirring devotion, an almost sensual yearning for physical possession, now in the dramatic experience of war takes on an unwonted appearance, sorrowful and afflicted, yet at the same time proud.

The transition from the early to the later Elytis may be traced not only contextually in the "Heroic Song" but also in some parts of the poems of "I kalosíni stis likopories" (Kindness in the Wolfpasses) and *The Axion Esti*. The first of these two, though published in 1946, draws its genesis from the atmosphere of war,[2] reproducing the conflict between opposing values where choice, though forced, is categorical and relatively easy. "Kindness" has to face the enemy with its own arms and give battle. And the poet has to accept the fact that he must bid farewell to the diversions and childish fancies that previously satisfied him. In the collision with reality, the dream-world in which his poetry had been submerged disintegrates into a nebula where fragments may still be seen of the old carefree simplicity, relived in the recalling of a legend.[3] An analogous situation is to be found in *The Axion Esti* ("The Passion," Psalm I, line 1 ff.). Here, too, the innocents are trapped with no way of escape. There is no alternative but to fight, each with his own weapons.[4] And in actual fact, when the Greeks have to face the brutal and absurd Fascist aggression, no man can any longer be tempted by idle recreation. Lethargy is jolted into action. Even the scenic background is abruptly transformed. Gone is the sea spray playing on shells and polished stones, gone is the splendor of light and color; now there are bloody battles on gloomy, snow-topped mountains. Elytis had already used these mountains in a poem in "Sun the First," in which he identified Greece with her bare and gloriously snowy peaks.[5] The scenery of the "Heroic Song" is full of mountains; even when they are not explicitly mentioned, their looming, solemn presence can be felt, protecting or threatening.

The "Heroic Song" is densely packed with emblematic values skillfully inserted into an organic, linear structure. The very title of the "song," with its two adjectives, encompasses the work's compound nature: something halfway between a threnody and a short epic poem. Of the threnody it has the lamentations, the pining regret, the exaltation of life passed by; it makes some use of formulae and modules taken from folk poetry, adapted to Elytis's own style and language. Of the epic poem it has the mythical fable-like quality, the wish to extract a cathartic teaching from the drama of the fallen soldier, the idealization of the protagonist. The lack of realistic tone in the poem is scarcely surprising, considering Elytis's esthetic conceptions. The situations are not wholly materialized; they are presented in brief glimpses, in impassioned suggestions evoked from the world of the unconscious.

The "Heroic Song" contains fourteen poetical compositions, each corresponding to a moment in the life—and death—of the extraordinary protagonist. These fourteen sections are not connected in time or place, but are interlinked through an inner affinity and through oneiric memory. The sections vary in both content and tone, leading to inevitable comparisons with a symphony.[6] One might also be put in mind of the various scenes of a dream-vision reproduced in a series of apparently disconnected film frames skillfully stitched together by a montage expert.

At least four main sequences may be distinguished in the poem: 1) the antefact, including sections I–II, which present the Greek-Albanian landscape in an ever-stronger foreboding of death, and section III, in which the outbreak of war is recounted; 2) the death of the protagonist (section IV); 3) the consequences of his death, including the poet's shock at what has happened (V–VI), the mother's desperation as seen against the background of the death scene (VII), the diminution of the entire world through the Second Lieutenant's death (VIII–X) and the punishment of those guilty of his death (XI); and 4) the transfiguration and resurrection of the fallen Second Lieutenant (XII, XIV), with an interpolated lament for his unfinished life (XIII).

Let us examine those sections most deserving of note. The first line ("There where the sun first dwelt")[7] of section I foretokens the drama in its re-evocation of the country scenery, which takes on a nostalgic connotation in the twofold reference to place and time, "there" and "first." The contrast with the present is strongly expressed in line 11, which begins with the adverb "now" (repeated in the next line), and initiates a series of somber, distressful images: the spreading shadow (l. 11) has now obscured the sun forever.

In section II the transformation is announced by the adverb "now," placed conspicuously as the first word of the first line: "Now in muddy waters an agitation arises." The waters are no longer still, as they were in line 14 of section I, and are no longer clear; *now* they are muddy because *now* there is agitation. The identity is, in fact, total: now = agitation. The trepidation for the morrow is well-rendered in the urgent series of impassioned metaphoric images.[8] The shattered peace of the countryside is contrasted with the soldiers' unwavering purpose, which is expressed in their war-cry, "fire or the sword."[9] The expression in lines 19–20, "Something evil / Shall flame up," returns in a slightly altered form in the penultimate line of section II, where it is no longer generic but is instead directed against a specific object, the aggressors.

The conflict becomes reality in section III, and man smiles in vain, indifferent to his destiny in the face of death, which approaches with the dull roar of the big guns and which leaves behind it destruction and smoke. All is plunged into darkness, despite the efforts of the sun to break through. The technical composition of this section differs from that of the others, which come in compact units of varying length (occasionally separated by single lines or couplets). Here there are six short three-line strophes, each containing a complete logical meaning or image. The last two strophes are exceptional in that they are linked, if only by the antithesis of day and night, the images which dominate the fifth and sixth strophes respectively.

The scene is dominated in section IV by the body of the fallen soldier, stretched out on "his scorched battle-coat."[10] The sudden presentation of the dead protagonist is unusual and extremely effective. The first two strophes are rich in original metaphors and similes, whose purpose is to convey the real meaning of the lieutenant's death. But the most powerful strophe is the third, depicting as if in a hasty uncompleted sketch[11] the lifeless figure, of which only a few clear details are presented: the empty helmet, the mud-soiled blood, the "half-finished" arm and especially the "small bitter well" boring into the forehead. The use of modular repetitions and refrains gives the final strophe the air of a funeral dirge.

In accordance with lamentation technique, the re-evocation in section VI opens on a mythical, legendary tone. Three long strophes develop the motif suggested by the first sentence of each.[12] Structurally the sentences follow the same pattern of verb-adjective-noun, the verb and noun remaining unchanged and the adjective always different: "He was a handsome lad," "He was a sturdy lad," "He was a valiant lad." While in the first two strophes the re-evocation recalls a distant, almost timeless age, the last, developing the opening and closing line, refers to his wartime experiences until his death. A series of metaphors gives another glimpse of the body, which is the "silent shipwreck of dawn"; the mouth is a "small songless bird," the hands "wide plains of desolation" (i.e., city squares). In section VII, two prosopopoeiae in the form of the female characters Suffering and Solitude (in the first and second strophes respectively) prepare the way for the highly emotive scene of the mother in mourning-weeds. Less convincing are the closing lines which overemphatically declare that it is the lot of mothers to weep[13] and of men to fight, almost implying that courage may be an end in itself, in contrast with the ideal values personified in the protagonist.

The eleventh section is divided into three strophes (the first two containing eleven lines each, the third containing three) and is devoted to the enemies, "Those who committed evil." Each of the three strophes starts with this isolated hemistich. Tormented and appalled at their evil-doing, the enemies vanish in a dark cloud. The second strophe has been rightly said to re-echo klephtic poetry,[14] though in a personal and of course modern way. It is true that some denunciations may seem too harsh, especially today, considering that they involve an entire country with no distinction between the political responsibilities of the leaders of the Fascist dictatorship and the Italian people, reluctantly forced into becoming aggressors toward a kindred people. However, this has little importance from the point of view of art. What is important is that these lines genuinely re-echo popular feeling prevalent in Greece at that tragic point in time, when the decision to defend to the death was taken not out of a sense of nationalistic hatred or antagonism but as an option for justice, liberty and democracy.

In the last three sections (XII–XIV) the hero ascends to heaven saluted by birds and men whom he recognizes as brothers in a cosmic embrace, while crystal bells herald the coming of Easter. The good and innocent[15] hero, dead *ante diem*, has redeemed himself by his sacrifice. Not only do his person and his tragedy belong to a higher sphere, but his country, too, is finer than all others. His country is the land where once the sun dwelt and where one day it will return to shine. It is the land of justice, the land of beauty, the land of passion. Elytis thus consciously and organically develops his ethical conception of Greece and Grecism, even though it is tied to a particular case chosen as a symbol of an historic moment. Later, in *The Axion Esti*, Elytis's magnum opus, he provides a further and more explicit structure, both diachronic and synchronic, of the most significant events and moments of the Greek world.[16]

As to the style and language of the "Heroic Song," a few remarks may suffice. On the whole, if we compare the poem with Elytis's previous and subsequent work, we find confirmation of the boldness of certain stylistic techniques and of the creative richness of his language. Among the most frequent stylistic devices, the metaphor is particularly noteworthy. Bearing in mind that Elytis's choice of language is instinctively disposed toward figurative uses, thus creating innumerable metaphors, only the most notable will be pointed out. Classifying them according to the two elements being compared,[17] these are: a) syntactically dependent metaphors (using the genitive in Greek) such as "famine of joy," "crumbs of heaven" and "branch of oblivion"; b) juxtaposed metaphors such as "hermit rocks," "gipsy anemones," "cloud months," "sickle moon" and "tomboy flowers"; c) appositional metaphors, including "garden, odeon of flowers" and "mouth, small bird"; and d) compound metaphors, such as *aloghóvouno* (mountain/horse), *sinefolíkena* (clouds/she-wolf), *nerantzokóritsa* (girls/bitter oranges) and *horiatomouzmouliá* (medlar-tree/peasant). Lexically there are some interesting linguistic formations, such as the compounds *foradhopoúles* (young mares), *thampóhrisa* (of tarnished gold), *ghalazovoló* (to irradiate with blue) and *iridhohtipiménos* (struck by the iris). Syntactically we encounter again a curious peculiarity of Elytis's language, namely, that of using an intransitive verb with an object in the accusative (as, for example, "a flag *flapped* aloft *earth and water*," "black centuries about him *bay* with skeletons of dogs *the hideous silence*"). These violations of the normal rules produce bizarre and powerful effects, which in the final analysis sustain the poet's tendency toward figurative language, enhancing his linguistic genius and his creative fantasy with unexpected properties.

[1] It must not be forgotten that the poet named the sun in the title of his collection "Sun the First," where the adjective is not a mere attribute but is intended to bring the symbol "sun" back to an absolute and primogenial value. From this conception, added to his physical attachment to nature, comes the expression "to drink sun," which he attributes to himself ("Sun the First," IV, 1); in *The Axion Esti*, "The Passion," I, 1, he defines himself as "sundrinker." For a like expression see also "Heroic Song," XII, 13.

[2] Like another poem, "The Albaniad," published in the review *Panspoudhastikí*, no. 41, 25 December 1962, pp. 11–14.

[3] This sort of flashback, recalling moments idealized in the memory, is an interesting technical device that we see used again in the "Heroic Song." Also interesting is the insistence on the goodness of the protagonist, who, like the Second Lieutenant of the "Heroic Song," symbolizes the entire Greek people summoned to the holocaust.

[4] The expression occurs three times in *The Axion Esti*—to be precise, twice in "Genesis" and once in "The Passion." In this last part there is a significant variant: he said," which in "The Genesis" parenthetically concludes the expression, becomes "I said" in "The Passion," emphasizing the poet's involvement.

[5] III, 15–16. Cf. on this point A. Karandonis,

Isaghoyí stí neóteri píisi, Athens, 1958, p. 212. The compound *khionódhoksa*, so typical of Elytis, may allude to the recent triumphs of the Albanian war; but it is significant that it also occurs in *The Axion Esti* ("The Passion," V, 22), in a passage celebrating Mount Pindus and Mount Athos (l. 5), as well as the mountainous nature of Greece in general (ll. 1–2).

[6] Regarding the various "times" in the poem, see the convincing arguments of M. Vitti, *Odisseo Elitis. Poesie*, Rome, 1952, p. 69.

[7] All quotations from the "Heroic Song" are taken from Kimon Friar's translation in *The Sovereign Sun*, Philadelphia, Temple University Press, 1974, pp. 87–97.

[8] See, for example, ll. 5–6: "Earth hides her stones / Fear digs a hole and scurries into it."

[9] The cry is a salute in answer (l. 12) to "those who set out with fire or with the sword" (l. 13). In *The Axion Esti* we find the expression "iron and fire" referred to the enemies' gifts ("The Passion," VII, 28 and 30; in l. 31 the expression is extended to "weapons and iron and fire").

[10] The first line "He lies down now on his scorched battle-coat" recurs twice more but without the adverb "now": after the first sudden reference to the body, necessitating a reference to time in order to indicate the passing from life to death, its presence is then indicated as an irreversible state.

[11] The fact that neither the face nor the person is

well-defined, far from being a shortcoming (as argued by G. Themelis, *I neóteri piísi mas*, Athens, 1963, p. 59), is a most felicitous device in full accord with Elytis's allusive technique. See also a significant analogy with the poem "Autopsy" from the collection "Six and One Remorses for the Sky," in *The Sovereign Sun*, p. 120.

[12] The three sentences have a metrically autonomous position, since the first occupies the first hemistich of the first strophe and the other two coincide respectively with the first line of the other two strophes.

[13] This assertion attracts somewhat pungent criticism from G. Kordatos, *Istoría tis neoellinikís loghotehnías*, Athens, 1962, p. 586.

[14] According to L. Politis, *Themata tís loghotehnías mas*, Athens, 1947, p. 88.

[15] The values he represents, in the manner of the heroes of Solomós (cf. A. Arghiriu, *Epitheor. Tehnis*, vol. 7, pamphlet 40, April 1958, p. 181), are constantly reiterated in the poem. See in particular VI, 35–36, "(They so easily reached into his brain / He who had never known evil)," and compare with the above-mentioned "Autopsy": "In his brain nothing but a shattered echo of the sky."

[16] The only critic, as far as I know, who has seen this unity of conception in Elytis is V. Nisiotis, ("Odhisseas Elítis. I sineídhisi tou ellinikoú míthou," *Kritikí*, vol. 3, pamphlets 13–14 [January-April 1961], p. 6), who recalls that the "Hellenic line" was an early aspiration of Elytis; he also very shrewdly points out (ibid., p. 5) that the "Heroic Song" is *The Axion Esti* in miniature. To avoid any possibility of misinterpretation, it must be made clear that the Greece of Elytis is not the fruit of nationalistic exaltation but, on the contrary, is meant to represent the sum of values having universal bearing.

[17] Occasionally the comparison takes the form of a simile of true classical structure, introduced by "as" or "like": "But the night half-rose like a trodden viper" (III, 16).

The Voices of Elytis's *The Axion Esti*

By EDMUND KEELEY

The response of Greek readers to Odysseus Elytis's most ambitious poem, *The Axion Esti*, has been ambivalent during the fifteen years since it appeared in Athens in late 1959 to end more than a decade of silence by a poet then considered to be Greece's best hope among the "younger" generation of poets to follow George Seferis.[1] Though the poem earned the First National Award for Poetry in 1960 and was widely read during the years that followed, the attitude of leading critics remained mixed. A similar ambivalence was also evident in the response of English-speaking readers to the two sections of the poem that appeared in this country and England during the 1960s.[2] For those brought up on the post–Eliot/Pound mode—or on the Cavafis/Seferis mode—the poem was seen to be excessively rhetorical and subjective, at times too obviously programmatic in its formal and thematic projections, at other times too obscure.

Given a commitment to these anti-rhetorical modes, one could find ample ground for regarding the poem as overblown in many of its parts, perhaps even in its central intentions. But this is not the only commitment that governs modern poetry, certainly not so in the case of the modern Greek tradition. Those readers familiar with twentieth-century Greek poetry can discern a direct line from the rhetorical modes of Palamás and Sikelianós to those of *The Axion Esti*, modes that are as characteristic of Greek verse in this century as the more frugal, controlled expression of Cavafis and Seferis. There is now increasing evidence in the response of English-speaking readers, particularly the younger poets in this country, that the poem speaks with power to those who turn (or return) to the surrealist movement of the early twentieth century for their principal inspiration.

My argument here is that there is no single mode in the poem but several modes and a variety of voices—some more objective and dramatic than others, some more effective than others, but serving to shape an impressive poetic statement in their totality—and that even the most subjective and rhetorical of the poem's voices really should be judged within a relevant context: that phase of the modern Greek tradition which foreshadows Elytis's use of an enlarged first-person, his most controversial voice. For those English-speaking readers without access to the work of Palamás and Sikelianós, it may be helpful to approach the poem not with reference to the post–Eliot/Pound mode but with reference to those poets in our tradition who engaged in an enterprise parallel to Elytis's, specifically Walt Whitman and Dylan Thomas. Both these poets project a first-person voice that usually manages to transcend the subjective and rhetorical trappings that come with it, sometimes in a manner that anticipates Elytis's first-person speaker in portions of *The Axion Esti*. When Whitman sings, in "Song of Myself, 16," that

> I am of old and young, of the foolish as much as the wise,
> Regardless of others, ever regardful of others,
> Maternal as well as paternal, a child as well as a man,

81

> Stuff'd with the stuff that is coarse and stuff'd with the stuff
>   that is fine,
> One of the Nation of many nations, the smallest the same and the
>   largest the same,
> A Southerner soon as a Northerner . . .

his large first-person voice is meant to rise above the subjective syntax and to speak for the nation, for the proposed national sensibility that the "I" is intended to represent; and it is partly the rhetorical tone of the passage that forces the reader to accept this grand design.

Elytis attempts the same kind of representation through his first-person speaker in several of the Psalms of part two, "The Passion," for example in Psalm III:

> RICHES you've never given me,
>   devastated as I've always been by the tribes of the Continents,
>   also glorified by them always, arrogantly![3]

or in Psalm V:

> MY FOUNDATIONS on mountains,
>   and the people carry the mountains on their shoulders
>   and on these mountains memory burns
>   like the unconsumed bush.

Here the first-person voice speaks for the nation more than for the self: those riches never given, and the devastation by "tribes of the Continents," are attributes that belong not so much to a personal as a national predicament; and "my foundations" become the country's foundations when the mountains that hold them are raised on the shoulders of "the people." The rhythm, as in Whitman, is that of a rhetorical progress from "I" as persona to "I" as metaphor for a general sensibility.

In those instances when Elytis's first-person voice speaks in a more overtly personal context, his mode appears closer to that of Dylan Thomas, whose work also reveals a parallel handling of imagery. The opening lines of Thomas's "Fern Hill," for example, remind us of lines in part one, "The Genesis":

> Now as I was young and easy under the apple boughs
> About the lilting house and happy as the grass was green,
>   The night above the dingle starry,
>   Time let me hail and climb
>   Golden in the heydays of his eyes,
> And honored among wagons I was prince of the apple towns
> And once below time I lordly had the trees and leaves
>   Trail with daisies and barley
> Down the rivers of the windfall light.

"The Genesis" opens as follows:

> IN THE BEGINNING the light And the first hour
>   when lips still in clay
>   try out the things of the world
>   Green blood and bulbs golden in the earth
>   And the sea, so exquisite in her sleep, spread
>   unbleached gauze of sky
>   under the carob trees and the great upright palms
>   There alone I faced
>   the world
>   wailing loudly

Both poets offer a persona who speaks out of personal past history, childhood in the case of Thomas and infancy in the case of Elytis. But the objective of this personal evocation is to provide a context for the creation of the brave new world that each persona discovers during the innocence of his early life. The focus is not on auto-biographical detail but on those elements that make the world surrounding the persona green and golden, before the progress of time intrudes to bring a consciousness of the fall from grace—the knowledge of death in Thomas and of evil in Elytis—that changes early Eden into the harsher world of later years. The subjective voice again serves a broader, metaphoric vision; the rhetorical tone, even the conceits ("prince of the apple towns," "unbleached gauze of sky") again seem appropriate in elevating the ordinary to the level of wonder, specifically, the wonder that comes with "trying out the things of the world" in a state of innocence.

These parallels illustrate two forms of the first-person voice in *The Axion Esti*, forms that fall between what Palamás called the personal and the temporal, or "lyricism of the *I*" and "lyricism of the *we*."[4] When Elytis allows the personal, or the self, to dominate the more general group consciousness, he is clearly less successful, as in Psalm X of "The Passion," where the persona's defensiveness under attack by "the young Alexandrians" seems to border on paranoia. And he is also less successful when his persona takes on the role of prophet, turning from the re-created world before him to visionary abstractions (e.g., "I see the coherence of secret meanings," or "Blessed, I say, are the potent ones who decipher the Undefiled"), as in passages of the Reading called "Prophetic" and in the late Psalms. The first-person voice appears inevitably to speak with the greatest conviction and force when it is discovering or celebrating or even challenging the symbols of "this small world the great" that are rooted in the Greek reality, whether of landscape, recent history or literary tradition—all of which evoke a shared, group response and therefore transcend the overly hermetic.

The same criterion applies to the first-person voice of the numerous intricate Odes of "The Passion," a voice that is in one sense the most subjective and rhetorical that we hear in *The Axion Esti* but that is at the same time the most formal, confined within the limits of a lyrical frame created by strict metrics and frequent refrains. It is a voice clearly meant to sing, and we permit it some of the license this intention presupposes. But again, to the extent that the rhetorical "I" of these Odes "takes the shape of my native country" (as the poet himself puts it in Ode j), it escapes an excess of self-consciousness and promotes some of the finest lyrics that Elytis has written. To the extent that it speaks privately or with a tone of self-righteousness ("Betrayed, I remained on the plain, alone, / Stormed, I was taken in the castle, alone, / The message I raised I endured alone!") or through slogans ("In the desolate and empty city / only the hand remains / To paint across the great walls / BREAD AND FREE-DOM") or in "prophetic" abstractions ("But then, at the sixth hour of the erect lilies, / When my judgment will make a crack in Time, / The eleventh Commandment will emerge from my eyes: . . ."), it rings rather hollow, the product not so much of the poet's mature, liberated spirit as of his programmatic attempt to present grand themes.[5]

A related esthetic can be brought to bear on the more objective voices that emerge in *The Axion Esti*, and they are several. One index of the sophistication of this poem, of the progress in method that occurred during the years of silence that preceded it, resides in the poet's "dramatic manner of expression" (to use the phrase Seferis offered in designating what he had learned first of all from reading Eliot's *The Waste Land*)[6] —an expression that often finds embodiment in characters some distance from the poet himself and his persona. The first such character to appear is "the One I really was, the One of many centuries ago, / the One still verdant in the midst of fire, the One still tied to heaven" in "The Genesis," a kind of alter ego who acts as the creator of the infant poet's green world. This voice utters some of the best lines in the poem, lines that are effective exactly because they evoke a recognizable landscape, a poetic image of Greek reality, while at the same time dramatizing the infant poet's emerging sensibility:

> And ample the olive trees
>   to sift the light through their fingers
>   that it may spread gently over your sleep
> and ample the cicadas
>   which you will feel no more
>   than you feel the pulse inside your wrist
> but scarce the water
>   so that you hold it a God and understand the meaning of its voice
> and the tree alone
>   no flock beneath it
>   so that you take it for a friend
>   and know its precious name
> sparse the earth beneath your feet
>   so that you have no room to spread your roots
>   and keep reaching down in depth
> and broad the sky above
>   so that you read the infinite on your own[7]

The experiment in dramatic expression extends, in "The Passion," to a series of prose poems called Readings, where the speaking voice is essentially that of a narrator, though the narrative focus shifts from the point of view of a participant in the action to that of a more distant observer and, finally, to that of the "poet-prophet" mentioned above. The voice is most alive in the early Readings, when Elytis succeeds in creating a tone that is organically related to his subject and to the image of experience he wishes to project, without the intrusion of explicitly subjective overtones. In the First and Second Readings, for example, the unidentified narrator, a soldier participating in the historical moments described (both during the Albanian campaign of 1940–41), speaks in a colloquial language that provides verisimilitude in that particular context and that also subtly echoes the colorful demotic of a great nineteenth-century narrator, General Makriyánnis, whose *Memoirs* described the Greek War of Independence and its aftermath. The relation of World War II to earlier Greek history in terms of an engaged perspective is thus established by narrative tone as much as by the kind of direct allusion—too direct for my taste—that invokes heroes out of the past to travel in the company of our contemporary soldiers. In the best of the Readings, tradition becomes an organic element of the language celebrating tradition.

The voice in the concluding section of the poem, "The Gloria," is perhaps the most consistently effective in *The Axion Esti*. Here the poet overtly assumes the stance of celebrant, but in general he allows the world he is celebrating to speak for itself. Except for the refrains "PRAISED BE" and "HAIL," he remains outside the context he projects, and the refrains simply establish a frame of intention, a celebrative tone, for his evocation of all that he finds in "this small world the great" which is most worthy of praise. The proof of worthiness is left to the images created, without any subjective pressure from poet or persona; the value of the world rendered depends on the degree to which we the readers find the various images of it convincing—and most of them prove to be so. This suggests a truly liberated strategy, one that serves to invoke the best of Elytis's early work but now reinforced by a mature command of plotting, of decorum and aptness in the progression from one image to the next, values sometimes slighted in the early Elytis. Perhaps more important, in some passages of this section, the poet succeeds—as his predecessor Seferis so often does—in conveying the mythological dimension that pervades the details of contemporary life in Greece without pressing the case through overt comment or allusion to literary sources. In the following passage, for example, gods and heroes from the Greek past are brought subtly into the contemporary landscape by way of a sudden metaphor linking a tree trunk with the goddess of fertility and vegetation who presumably animates it, by way of a compound epithet, and a name carrying echoes of Homer, and the intermingled whispering of deities and the natural element they inhabit, all made to seem casually at home in the island world that the poet is celebrating:

> The white and porous middle of day
> the down of sleep lightly ascending
>> the faded gold inside the arcades
> and the red horse breaking free

> Hera of the tree's ancient trunk
> the vast laurel grove, the light-devouring
>> a house like an anchor down in the depths
> and Kyra-Penelope twisting her spindle

> The straits for birds from the opposite shore
> a citron from which the sky spilled out
>> the blue hearing half under the sea
> the long-shadowed whispering of nymphs and maples

Throughout most of this final section of the poem, Elytis is observing first of all, observing and re-creating, selecting details that will move the reader to a recognition and letting any attendant thematic or ideological overtones come as they may. The picture is all, and when it is right, it can startle the reader with a new perspective on the hauntingly familiar:

> PRAISED BE the wooden table
> the blond wine with the sun's stain
>> the water doodling across the ceiling
> the philodendron on duty in the corner . . .

> PRAISED BE the heatwave hatching
> the beautiful boulders under the bridge
>> the shit of children with its green flies
> a sea boiling and no end to it . . .

> THE ISLANDS with all their minium and lampblack
> the islands with the vertebra of some Zeus
>> the islands with their boat yards so deserted
> the islands with their drinkable blue volcanoes

The only faltering in "The Gloria" is that which we have seen in other sections: a weakness for vague abstraction in those few moments when the poet attempts to rise above the world before him to the region of absolutes and general principles. In the closing lines of this section, he juxtaposes representations of the "Now" and the "Forever" in a sort of coda to the whole poem. Neither plane, as rendered here, moves the heart or even the mind to the kind of discovery effected by the specific images we have seen. And this rhetorical mode of evocation serves to diffuse and intellectualize what has so far been poetically concrete:

> Now the hallucination and the mimicry of sleep
> Forever forever the word and forever the astral Keel
>
> Now the moving cloud of lepidoptera
> Forever the circumgyrating light of mysteries
>
> Now the crust of the Earth and the Dominion
> Forever the food of the Soul and the quintessence ...
>
> Now the amalgam of peoples and the black Number
> Forever the statue of Justice and the great Eye ...

The poem ends: "and Forever this small world the Great!" Indeed. But as the best passages in the poem demonstrate, the eternal dimensions of this small world are most convincingly established when the greatness of it is celebrated with a lower case "g." This is the poet's strongest impulse in the poem, and it is what makes *The Axion Esti* both a major stage in the poet's development and a major contribution to the modern Greek tradition in poetry.

---

[1] Yannis Ritsos, who has now emerged as the other distinguished heir, was still suffering at that time from either unpremeditated ignorance on the part of the Greek literary establishment or what some have seen as a politically motivated conspiracy that prevented his just recognition.

[2] "The Genesis" in *Poetry*, October 1964, and "The Gloria" in *Agenda*, Winter 1969, both translated by Edmund Keeley and George Savidis.

[3] The translations used in this essay are from the bilingual edition of *The Axion Esti*, Edmund Keeley and George Savidis, trs., Pittsburgh, University of Pittsburgh Press, 1974.

[4] See Robinson's illuminating discussion of *My Poetic* in "Greece in the Poetry of Costis Palamas," *Review of National Literatures*, Fall 1974, pp. 42 ff.

[5] An outline of Elytis's program, taken from his unpublished commentary on the poem, is offered in the Notes to the bilingual edition of *The Axion Esti*, p. 152.

[6] *On the Greek Style: Selected Essays in Poetry and Hellenism*, Rex Warner and Th. Frangopoulos, trs., Boston, 1966, p. 167.

[7] From the third "hymn."

1979 Nobel Laureate Odysseus Elytis: From *The Axion Esti* to *Maria Neféli*

By M. BYRON RAIZIS

In the course of their development most major writers "grow" and pleasantly surprise their readers who enjoy perceiving this horizontal, vertical or internal growth. The spiritual dimensions of their work also increase with each new creation, and the newer often acquires a philosophic quality and an aura of profundity that earlier texts lacked. This observation is particularly true of Odysseus Elytis, who constantly grew and renewed, or refreshed, his poetry ever since the *Prosanatolizmí* (Orientations) of his vibrant youth in 1939. But what could this Greek poet achieve after *The Axion Esti*—which in 1959 had established him, along with George Seferis and Yannis Ritsos, as a Poet of his Nation—to prove that as an artist he was still alive and well and growing in new directions, achieving additional dimensions? The answer is the poetry of *Maria Neféli* some twenty years later.

In this book Elytis has grown in all the aforementioned directions and, above all, internally. The strange "newness" of *Maria Neféli* should not surprise or offend us, for we must try to comprehend and appreciate it in terms of his artistic work as a whole. The Poet actually prepares us for such a reaction by attaching two significant epigraphs to his book. The first, borrowed from the Gospel according to Matthew (5:39), commands the faithful: "But I say unto you, That ye resist not evil." The second, taken from his own "Orientations," also commands us to "Guess, labor, feel: On the other side I am the same." So this newest collection is still the spiritual offspring of the same poet, the artist of the Greek sun, the luminous Aegean, and of love and "splendor in the grass." At the same time, following the spirit of the Evangelist, Elytis warns and commands us not to resist evil, not to fight back in anger, not to become violent when offended. The rest of the Gospel verse adds: "But whosoever shall smite thee on the right cheek, turn to him the other also."

In his often cited interview with Ivar Ivask back in 1975, reprinted in this book, Elytis had talked of three periods in his poetry. The first consists of "Orientations" and the collections that were produced during the hard and dark years of the 1940s. After a rather long silence appeared *The Axion Esti* (1959) and the "memory" poems from his experiences in World War II and its traumatic aftermath. In these poems of his second period a mature Elytis directly and indirectly alludes to, and employs, historic and cultural details from Greece's recent as well as Byzantine past. The third period contains his books of verse of the 1970s, his prose works and *Maria Neféli*. As he puts it himself, Elytis is not quite sure that *Maria Neféli* "constitutes a kind of *summa* of my third period just as *The Axion Esti* stands out from my second period." He adds, though, that *Maria Neféli* perhaps does "constitute the synthesis of my third period which is already finished in my mind."[1]

In the same interview Elytis explains the basic concepts of this composition, which was then work in progress. Unlike most of the poems which, though "usually rooted" in his experience, "do not directly transcribe actual events," *Maria Neféli* was inspired by a young woman he had met in real life. His contact with this attractive, liberated, restless or even blasé representative of today's young women made him suddenly desire "to write something very different from *The Axion Esti.*" This Maria then is the newest manifestation of the eternal female, the most recent mutation of the female principle which, in the form of Marina, Helen and other more traditional figures, had haunted the quasi-idyllic and erotic poems of his two earlier periods.

It must also be stressed that Maria is a product and *spiritus loci* of an urban environment. She has gone through experiences similar to those that had generated the lyrics of the Aegean climate and "The Sovereign Sun." Other experiences, though, as well as social developments and pressures, have left their imprint on her, completely obliterating the natural suntan. This urban Neféli is the offspring, not the sibling, of the women of Elytis's youth. Her setting is the polluted city, not the open country and its islands of purity and fresh air.

*

The spirit of the 1970s is very different indeed from that of the late 1950s and most of the 1960s, especially in Greece, where the oppressive military regime of 1967–74 had stifled all dissent and particularly the natural reactions of Greece's youth, who were experiencing a restless fermentation comparable to those of university students of the 1960s in America, in May 1968 France and elsewhere. The fall of the Junta in 1974 released all manner of pent-up emotions in the population. The most rebellious segment of the frustrated nation, the educated young, dramatized their differences with the world of their elders by means of political, pro-leftist activities. The more sophisticated, and the psychologically more complex or confused, expressed attitudes comparable to those of nonconformists and hippies in terms of life-style and social, or rather unsocial, orientation and ideology. The most radical and vociferous among the latter were the young women who, in addition to the malaise of the boys, had many more axes to grind on account of the treatment they had traditionally received from family and society because of their status as the "weak" sex under "protection." The persona of Maria Neféli is then the living embodiment of that kind of girl. She acts as an instigator of reactions on the part of the Poet. She is a catalyst that forces the Responder to confront situations and issues which without her he might have preferred to ignore, or to view them from an entirely different angle. Elytis's involvement with this contemporary Eve of the city inspired and nurtured the book that received her name as its telling title.

In its first edition (1978) *Maria Neféli* was described, and subtitled, a *skinikó píima*—that is, a dramatic or theatrical poem, meant for stage production. The third edition in 1979, however, has dropped this explanation or designation, because the Poet probably did not wish it to be mistaken for some sort of experimental theatre form, or a lyrical drama. On the contrary, he seems to suggest that epic and lyric parts are equally important in this multifaceted collage which depicts the landscape of the 1970s. The three-dimensional and composite form of *Maria Neféli* is such that a musician, a performer, a choreographer, even a stage designer may be challenged to turn it into a "show," a live artistic "happening" that is much more than a text to be read or heard. In these respects *Maria Neféli* is akin to the celebrated *Axion Esti*, which as composer Mikis Theodorakis has proven, is much more than a graet poetic text.

The main feature in the structure of *Maria Neféli* is the dialogue, or more precisely, a juxtaposition of parallel statements by its two dramatic characters, Maria Neféli and the Antifonitís (Responder), who stands for the Poet himself, as Elytis has indicated in the already mentioned interview. Neither character is stereotyped, simple or flat. Both are sophisticated and complex urbanites and express themselves in a wide range of styles, moods, idioms and stanzaic forms.

The first poem in the book, "The Presence," is the closest thing to a dramatic exchange between the two protagonists—for the Poet is as much a key figure here as the woman herself—and acts as an introduction to the book. Its lyrical prose and verse are followed by seven poems, each with its title, spoken by Maria. All seven are introduced by the phrase "Maria Neféli says," which serves as a stage direction, as it were. Maria's poems are printed in italics. En face are printed (in normal Roman type) seven corresponding poems spoken by the Responder (Poet), each with its title and each responding or existing parallel to each of Maria's pieces. At the bottom of the last page of each Neféli and Responder poem Elytis has appended an epigrammatic dictum (of one to three lines)—a total of fourteen—most of which are of remarkable economy, wisdom and beauty. "The Song of Maria Neféli," a light, fast-moving, autobiographical lyric in rhyming quatrains, concludes Part A of the book.

Part B repeats the same pattern, the only difference being that the Poet's seven pieces are printed first, followed by their seven epigrams; and these are faced by Neféli's seven responses (always in italics) and their epigrammatic codas. "The Song of the Poet," a candid confessional poem in rhyming couplets, completes Part B. Its last couplet could be rendered freely as: "That's why I sent my fate to hell / and returned to myself, to my shell." The third and last Part C restores Neféli as the first speaker. Her seven lyrics and their epigrams are countered by the Poet's seven pieces and their epigrams. The final poem in this part, "The Eternal Wager," serves as a kind of epilogue to the whole composition.

Readers familiar with the structure of *The Axion Esti*, "The Monogram," "Six and One Remorses for the Sky" and most longer and composite poems of Elytis will easily realize that the structure of *Maria Neféli* is an ingenious architectural variation based on similar principles and numbers of symbolic or mystical significance. Three and seven, Elytis's favorite numbers, are reflected in the tripartite organization of the book (Parts A, B and C), plus the seven poem-speeches by each of the two "actors." The number of the trinity is also reflected by the three lyrics that conclude the three parts. Seven and its multiples fourteen and twenty-one are respectively reflected in the number of poems by each person in every part (7), in the number of poems in each part (14), and in the total number of speeches by each person (21) in the whole of *Maria Neféli*. Elytis's predilection for the number seven may be explained by the fact that the Pythagoreans considered it the symbol of justice. Both speakers do justice to their views by airing them seven times on each of three occasions.

Kimon Friar has meticulously discussed the role and significance of these numbers in the structure and function of "The Monogram,"[2] so I need not belabor a point that careful Elytis fans are not likely to miss. After this brief outline of the poem's structural pattern, we may proceed with an examination of characters, themes, diction and style, and then attempt an evaluation of the whole.

*

Neféli in Greek means "cloud," a word that Aristophanes had used in his comedy *Nephelae* (*The Clouds*)—*nebulae* in Latin. Its connotations are many. A *neféli* is light, airy, foggy and floats in the sky changing shape and appearance following the whims of the winds. In Greek mythology Nephele was the mother of Phrixos and Helle, also the cloud of sadness and of death. In contemporary reality the word also applies to the cloud of air pollution that covers Athens and most big cities. It is also a fine net to catch birds, modern human birds dwelling in an Aristophanic city of birds in the clouds.[3] In the Christian tradition a *neféli* often surrounds an angel, or describes the space where the divine dwells—something that makes a precious or holy image remote, barely visible, almost inaccessible. Finally, a *neféli* (cloud) is by definition intangible and mysterious. I do not mean to say that Elytis had all these in mind when he thought of Maria Neféli. The fact remains, however, that its meaning suggests plenty.

The first name also, Maria, must have been chosen with care. Maria is the name of Christ's mother, the only traditional mother figure whose significance in the formulation of our moral values, and the restoration of hope after Eve's transgression, is universally accepted in the West. Maria is also the commonest name for a woman in Greece and much of the Christian world. So the combination of "Maria" and "Neféli" makes a very strong mixture indeed. At the same time the qualities suggested by "Neféli" are almost diametrically opposed to those of "Maria." The young woman and lover of today is all of these. Her complexity parallels the complexity of our social and metaphysical predicaments.

"Antifonitís" (Responder), used for the Poet, is equally carefully picked. In classical Greek *antifónesis* (or *antifónema*) means "response to an address," and in church terminology *antifonía* is the reciprocal chanting of biblical verses (*antífona*) by two alternating choirs. The word is of the same root as *diafonía* (disagreement), but the meaning is different. Elytis very wisely chose "Antifonitís" to suggest his role in the poem, because his attitude is closer to that of a commentator rather than to a disagreeing opponent in an argument. *Maria Neféli* could be taken as a modern Frostian "lover's quarrel with the world," since these two love and care about each other, and their differences arise from the way they react to external stimuli offered by society.

In poem 2 of Part A the Responder longs to become a *Nefelegerétes* (Cloud-Gatherer) like Zeus, the lover of mythological Nephele. And in "Hymn in Two Dimensions" of Part B he confesses his "two-dimensional" love for the girl. In several other pieces his admiration of her physical appearance is implied, while in others he sounds ironic or challenged by her behavior, manners and much of what she stands for.

These two characters, antithetical as they are, complete rather than negate each other. They coexist and constitute a "whole," not a system based on a Hegelian dialectic, to be sure, but on an antiphonal device like the reciprocal chanting in the church. Both choirs sing of similar or related events, wonders and values; but each utters its own words, to its own tune. Neither is more important, and both aim at the same goal. Paradoxically, though their courses are parallel and never converge, at the end both reach the same destination. This principle dominates meaning and form in *Maria Neféli*. Its themes and truths are complementary, and so are its organic parts.

In her first poem, "The Forest of Men," in a series of allusions to scientific names of flora, fauna and primitive creatures and men, Maria suggests the ferocity and jungle-like quality of the milieu where she breathes and functions. In that spirit she invites, or challenges, the Poet to follow her and adjust his behavior to the demands of that environment. The verse used is free but controlled. The epigram following her poem reads: "The law that I am / will not subdue me," thus asserting her independence. The response of the Poet, though apologetic, is positive. He accepts to follow Neféli, alluding to the failure of the world he had believed in, and to the necessity of substituting the primitive for the refined.

> Poetry, oh my Saint—forgive me
> but it is necessary to stay alive
> to cross to the other bank;
> everything is preferable
> to my slow murder by the past.

This is clearly a Poet's apologia. He feels doubts about the reality of his own existence, as well as of that of "The Light Tree," the "idol" which in the eponymous collection of 1971 had become a luminous symbol of his metaphysical salvation as an artist.

The meaning of this poem's title ("To stígma") is intentionally ambiguous, I believe. The word *stígma* in Greek may be the singular of *stígmata*, the holy marks that appeared on the palms of St. Francis of Assisi (who is mentioned in the title of Neféli's last poem in Part B), symbolizing the Saint's empathy with Christ's crucifixion. Offering this interpretation, Gina Politi writes: "The key word here is *Ananghelía* (Announcement). If the stigma is sin, it is also the seal of God, the promise of salvation by the angel bearing the news to Mary. The stigma connects the Antifonitís to another poet who received the stigmata, . . . St. Francis of Assisi."

This observation makes considerable sense in view of the context. Since, however, Elytis used the word *Ananghelía* instead of *Evanghelismós*, which is precisely the Greek for "Annunciation," one may suggest a parallel meaning which is quite secular and does not bestow on Elytis either the crown of suffering and sainthood or the Byronic stigma of Cain's sin. *To stígma* in Greek also means "the bearings," the navigational term indicating the point where longitude and latitude meet. The "Announcement" then may refer to the need felt by the Poet of "Orientations" to reorient himself, to avoid getting lost in "the forest of men" where he must follow Maria Neféli. Addressing her, he raises his reversed palm with open fingers forming "a heavenly flower," as he says, but also making the blasphemous gesture known as *múndza*, and adds: "We might have called this 'Hubris' or even a 'Star.'" This Hubris-Star may give him his bearings, for he concludes addressing his friends this time: "Don't make fun of my clumsiness / for you know that these are contrary times." Through this apologetic statement and gesture of disrespect toward the sky, the Poet is probably accounting for the strange novelties that his fans will encounter in *Maria Neféli*. The Poet guided by this "Hubris-Star" is not exactly the "sun-drinking"[4] Elytis of the refulgent Aegean, or the inspired maker of *The Axion Esti*. He is an artist who must always change his means and manners to survive as an artist *of today*—in other words, to avoid repeating, and thus dating, himself and his work. The epigram to his poem reads: "Show such dexterous clumsiness / and lo: God appears!" Its paradox explains Elytis's predicament and, at the same time, indicates the new and only way left for survival.

The six remaining poems of Neféli bear the titles "The Cloud," "Patmos," "Discourse on Beauty," "Through the Mirror," "The Thunder Steers" and "The Trojan War." The corresponding pieces of the Poet are "The Cloud-Gatherer," "The Revelation," "The Water Drop," "Aegeis," "Hymn to Maria Neféli" and "Helen." Without having to analyze each in detail, we may note the relation of each pair of poems even on the basis of what is suggested by their titles. To "The Cloud," which stands for Neféli herself, the Poet responds with his "Cloud-Gatherer," connoting Zeus the lover of Nephele. "Patmos" and "The Revelation" are, respectively, the island where St. John lived and died plus the title of his holy text, *The Apocalypse*. "The Water Drop" of the Responder, a thing of beauty and precious coolness in today's spiritual aridity, counters Neféli's "Discourse on Beauty." "Through the Mirror," a title written in English, implying the border of transition to the realm of irreality where the nebulous girl struggles to find herself, is countered by the Poet's "Aegeis," which, in addition to reminding us of the Aegean milieu, is actually the geologically primeval land whose vestiges haunt the dreams and longings of the Responder. "The Thunder Steers" is a kind of self-analysis by Neféli; the Poet counters it with his own "Hymn to Maria Neféli," whom he perceives as an Iris inhabiting our mundane world. The two final poems are about human conflict. Maria concludes hers with the telling line, "Each period has its own Trojan War." The Poet cleverly reciprocates with "Each period has its own Helen," emphasizing the cause rather than the result.

This statement-counterstatement device and technique introduces a motif. At the ends of "The Inquisition" and its response, "St. Francis of Assisi," both in Part B, we read: "Each period has its Inquisition" and "Each period has its own St. Francis of Assisi." At the ends of "Stalin" and "The Hungarian Insurrection," both in Part C, we find respectively: "Each period has its Stalin" and "Each period has its Hungarian insurrection." The repetition of this device strengthens the structure of the antiphonal composition and reiterates main thematic premises. I must also point out that this motif is always used in the seventh pair of poems in each part. Analogous stylistic and verbal motifs control other pairs of poems in all subdivisions and units of *Maria Neféli*. Nothing is disorganized or at random in this text about our contemporary confusion, disorientation, almost chaos.

The space of this article does not allow the luxury of discussing several lyrics in detail, as their complexity and sophistication—to say nothing of their poetic beauty—warrant. I will therefore mention their titles, hoping that even through them the reader not only will notice their organic interrelationship but will also form an idea on the range and order of themes that the two "actors" dramatize in their poems. In Part B the Antifonitís recites the following: "Pax San Tropezana" (*sic* in the original), "The Manual," "The Ancestral Paradise," "Eau de Verveine" (*sic* in the text), "Upper Tarquinia," "Hymn in Two Dimensions" and "The Inquisition." Neféli responds with "The Planet Earth," "Every Moon Confesses," "The Kite," "Discourse on Purity," "The Eye of the Locust," "Declaration Under Oath" and "St. Francis of Assisi." In Part C Neféli recites "Good Morning Sadness," "The Poets," "The Twenty-Four-Hour Life," "Discourse on Justice," "Electra Bar," "Djenda" and "Stalin." The Responder reciprocates with "Morning Exercises," "What Convinces," "The Life-Lasting Moment," "Naked Study," "Parthenogenesis," "Ich Sehe Dich" and "The Hungarian Insurrection."

The already mentioned final poem by Neféli, "Stalin," is obviously composed in rhyming couplets to be epigrammatic and dogmatic in its communication of her rejection of all political and religious dogma. Asserting that "the many falsify the One"—religious or political savior—she concludes paraphrasing a line from fairy tales about man-eating Giants and Dragons: "When you hear 'order' / it smells of human flesh." This way she alludes to the 1967 slogans of the Colonels in Greece. The Poet reciprocates by interpreting her words as "The One falsifies the many." He then ends his speech with the significant epigram: "Die if you must / but first seek to become the first cock / in Hades." This allusion, which is also found in Yeats's masterpiece "Byzantium," connotes faith and hope. According to the early Christian tradition the cock in Hades is a symbol of resurrection; its crowing will herald the time of rebirth for the deserving.

Similarly ethical in spirit, rather than merely optimistic and hopeful, is the last poem in the book, "The Eternal Wager," which, being addressed to the woman, is spoken by the Poet. It consists of seven oracular stanzas of three lines each—again the mystic numbers seven and three—and refers to the future, to the time when an aged Maria Neféli will have achieved the wisdom and peace that Odysseus Elytis has already reached. The Poet wagers "That one day you will sink your teeth / into the new lemon and will release / enormous quantities of sun from within it." And the last stanza concludes *Maria Neféli* by creating a beautiful picture worthy of the sensitive "sun-drinking" painter and poet: "That at last on your own you will gradually / become harmonized to the splendor / of sunrise and of sunset."

What we have mentioned can only give a fleeting impression of the poetic wealth and contemporary thematic relevance that abound in Elytis's latest collage of words and rhythms. Impressive is also the array of verse forms he uses: fine rhyming couplets, as well as parody couplets with intentionally clumsy or facile rhymes; quatrains and other kinds of stanzas with alternating rhymes, half-rhymes or internal ones; controlled or loose free verse; lyric prose and prosaic, almost vulgar verse. The variety of styles is astonishing: whole poems or passages are dramatic, narrative, lyric, satiric, oracular, contemplative or confessional. The tone changes according to the thematic demands of each poem, from serious to light, from humorous and ironic or sarcastic to didactic. Moods in the verbal expression suggest the ever-changing moods of volatile Neféli, and of the challenged or even agonized Poet.

His language is, clearly, more elaborate and difficult than the lingo of the nebulous woman. For the first time in his career Elytis uses much unpoetic diction, even profanities and abusive terms. Cabron's word (*skatá* in Greek) is not spared either. Phrases or even whole lines in some poems are written in German, Italian, English or French. Foreign names, titles and terms are always in their original languages—this linguistic mosaic in explosion must, of course, correspond to the cacophony of tourists and jet-set Greeks heard in the streets of downtown Athens. Strangely, as people become increasingly multilingual, their talk becomes more and more incoherent and less articulate— just functional. How does all this sound to the ears of a veteran master of the Greek language? *Maria Neféli* itself embodies the answer to this question.

All manner of allusions are found in this book: scientific, geographic, religious, artistic, literary, mythological, cultural, biblical, historical, contemporary, even commercial—all of them expertly utilized to create a keen commentary on today's life-style, esthetics, ideology, love, human relationships, philosophies and metaphysics by the two interacting persons in *Maria Neféli*. The trade names of cars, perfumes, cigarettes, gasoline, alcoholic drinks, air-lines—the universal words in today's "uniworld"—are used by Elytis, and are even made to have meaning and rhyme with his colloquial Greek. No translation can approximate this unique phenomenon. For my readers' sake I will transliterate two Greek lines that form couplets with two "international" ones to offer a small sample (from the Responder's "Ich Sehe Dich" [I See You]) of what this book consists of:

> m' astrapís amáxi tha se pári
> SAAB   MERCEDES   FERRARI
> skízondas tis prosópsis paleón spitión
> NESCAFÉ   LINGUAPHONE.
>
> (He will take you in a lightning car
> Saab Mercedes Ferrari
> Tearing the façades of old houses
> Nescafé Linguaphone.)

Last but not least, Elytis occasionally echoes or paraphrases ideas and images from his own poems "The Light Tree," "The Stepchildren" and other old or recent collections, thus reminding his readers that the father of *Maria Neféli* is a renewed and reoriented Elytis of *The Axion Esti*, of "Six and One Remorses for the Sky," of "The Concert of Hyanciths" and so on. This Elytis has grown and has learned to accept the good and the evil, light and darkness, ugliness and beauty, not as conflicting phenomena or values, but as coexisting and necessary manifestations in a realistic, complex urban world from which transcendence can be attempted only by means of what he calls "solar metaphysics."

*

Maria Neféli has had three consecutive editions within a year since its appearance, all of them before the awarding of the Nobel Prize to Odysseus Elytis. This attests to its popularity, especially among younger readers of poetry. Some academicians and critics of the older generation still want to cling to the image and concept of the "sun-drinking" Elytis of the Aegean spume and breeze and of the monumental *Axion Esti*, so they approach *Maria Neféli* with cautious hesitation as an experimental and not-so-attractive creation of rather ephemeral value. Younger reviewers and writers, however, are unanimously enthusiastic. Gina Politi writes: "I believe that *Maria Neféli* is one of the most significant poems of our times, and the response to the agony it includes *is written*; this way it saves for the time being the language of poetry and of humaneness." Poet and translator Nana Issaia agrees without reservation.[5] Reviewer Kostas Stamatiou asserts that "after the surprise of a first reading, gradually the careful student discovers beneath the surface the *constants* of the great poet: faith in surrealism, fundamental humanism, passages of pure lyricism."[6] The Italian neo-Hellenist Mario Vitti approaches the poem as an expert sociologist and historian of Greek culture and pronounces it self-sufficient, panoplied and needing no interpreters to become a possession of the public whose experiences it shares and records in a fresh poetic form that still bears the unmistakable "signature" of its unaged and renewed composer.[7]

My personal feeling is that *Maria Neféli* is, beyond doubt, the *summa* of Elytis's third creative period. And this original, dynamic and impressive poetic collage records and dramatizes the anguish and tragicomedy, the promise and vulgarity of our aggressive and incoherent decade, just as successfully as the *summa* of his second period, *The Axion Esti*, had distilled and preserved the agony and the glory of its own times.

University of Athens

[1] "Odysseus Elytis on His Poetry—From an Interview with Ivar Ivask" above. All subsequent Elytis statements cited here come from this interview unless otherwise noted.

[2] Odysseus Elytis, *The Sovereign Sun: Selected Poems*, Kimon Friar, tr. & ed., Philadelphia, Temple University Press, 1974, pp. 38–41.

[3] Some of these details were first mentioned by Gina Politi in her review of *Maria Neféli* in the daily newspaper *Kathimeriní* of 1 March 1979. Subsequent references to remarks by Politi are taken from this review. All translations are my own unless otherwise indicated. An English version of *Maria Neféli* by A.

Anagnostopoulos is scheduled by Houghton Mifflin for publication in late 1980.

[4] "The Sun-Drinking Elytis" (Athens, Ermías, 1971), a monograph in Greek by Lily Zoghráfou, echoes Elytis's title "Drinking the Corinthian Sun" from *Ílios o prótos* (Sun the First).

[5] Nana Issaia, in an interview with me on 29 December 1979 in her Athens apartment.

[6] Kostas Stamatiou, in a review published in the daily *Ta Nea* of 20 January 1979.

[7] Mario Vitti, in a short article in *Ta Nea*, 9 December 1979.

Notes on the "Open Book" of Odysseus Elytis

By THEOFANIS G. STAVROU

Odysseus Elytis's national and international reputation as a poet has, until recently, obscured the fact that he is also an accomplished prose writer and a sensitive critic. In Greece, to be sure, his column in the Athens newspaper *Kathimerini*, where he served as a regular critic for a time, his occasional articles in *Nea Ghrámmata* and other literary journals, as well as his monographic study on the Greek painter Theófilos (1973), established him as a perceptive "commentator" whose voice has left its creative mark on Greek culture, especially on literature and art. Still, both in Greece and abroad, Elytis is primarily known as the sun poet and the author of *The Axion Esti*.

The publication in late 1974 of Elytis's *Anihtá hártia* or "Open Book" (literally "Open Papers") promises to effect a balance in the author's reputation and place him alongside other major Greek literary figures, such as George Seferis, who excelled and have been recognized both as poets and prose writers. "Open Book" is undoubtedly one of the most significant volumes in the flood of publications which followed the end of military rule in Greece. Its 516 pages consist of an impressive collection of essays and "texts," many of them never published before, written over a period of four decades and reworked carefully between 1963 and 1966, and dealing with esthetic matters pertinent to modern European and especially to modern Greek culture. Despite Elytis's "confession" that he is neither a critic nor a prose writer, the "Open Book" demonstrates that he is both. He has certainly succeeded in proving that the modern Greek language has come into its own and is capable of expressing the most complete thoughts and of painting the most subtle scenes. The same wealth of striking images so characteristic of Elytis's poetry is readily noticeable in his prose as well. The book is, in some respects, a landmark in the intellectual and cultural history of modern Greece and most likely will remain a major reference work for many years to come, one which no serious neo-Hellenist can afford to ignore. It is hoped that the following comments and the translated excerpts presented elsewhere in this issue will serve as an introduction to this most useful volume.

The question of the versatility of the modern Greek language is as good a place as any to begin when considering Elytis's prose. In a way, this is of course a restatement of the problem of loyalty to one's native language, probably the most honorable if not the ultimate loyalty of all. Thanks to the loyalty of writers like Elytis and Seferis, modern Greek, through a process of synthesis incorporating its finest traditional elements from classical times to the present and through an imaginative response to the demands of the modern world, has reached a respectable level of expression; and precisely because it possesses such historical depth and unity, it occupies a unique position among European languages and is capable of extraordinary performance at different scales. Elytis's total commitment to his native language—which is such that he would like to wake up one morning and hear even the birds singing in Greek—is only part of the "Hellenolatry" so prominent in his work. At a time when such an attitude could easily be mistaken for parochialism, narrow or petty nationalism or even backwardness, Elytis prays for the emergence of five or ten Greek poets of the stature of Dionysios Solomós, who would attract readers to modern Greek the way Pindar and Sappho attracted them to classical Greek. This commitment stems partly from his conviction that the poet or the artist should not avoid dealing with basic truths simply because these have lost all meaning in our modern age. Instead, through his creative imagination he should seek to activate them within the context of contemporary reality.

Understandably, the main value of the "Open Book" is that it illuminates Elytis's poetic work by putting it in its geographical and cultural setting. It also sketches the sources of his inspiration and training and charts the evolution of his artistic expression. Some of the passages from the introductory part, such as "The Radiance of Youth," "Love in Poetry" and "Death the First Truth," as well as larger essays like "Girls and Dreams," are in a way perceptive commentaries on Elytis's poetry, which has immortalized youth, the life-giving Greek sun and the dazzling Aegean. As he himself epigrammatically put it: "I have perceived myself somewhere between a sea rising from the little whitewashed wall of a church and a barefooted girl whose dress is lifted by the wind, a fortunate moment, which I struggle to capture and for which I lie in wait with Greek words." What Kimon Friar correctly observed about Elytis's poetry on this subject applies equally to some of his prose and critical essays: "Elytis created a Mediterranean land and myth in which his boys and girls can live a life not as it is but as they wish it to be, although nostalgically touched and corroded with the taints of reality." More significantly, however, throughout Elytis's prose as throughout his poetry there persists a distinctive attitude toward the reality of a world which in the twentieth century has known dehumanization and destruction. Like Matisse, Elytis sought through his art to counterbalance the horror and evil in our time, a stupendous effort which has frequently been misunderstood and characterized as "optimism." Elytis pursued this faith in his art uncompromisingly, refusing to allow the pressures of his epoch to distort him or make him servile, for he believes that "the poet is a cutting edge of the moral and the real world" and that poetic accomplishments along with political struggles for social liberation will bring about a special kind of justice. Thus oscillating between theory and practice in his "Open Book," Elytis weaves a complex but highly useful system reflecting his world view as well as the guiding principles of his art.

At the same time, the "Open Book" provides authoritative statements on some of the major issues which continue to have considerable impact on modern Greek culture and society. Without being didactic, it seeks to set the record straight in a confused situation where precise definitions have lost their honorable place. This Elytis accomplishes through his "texts," which from the point of view of the cultural historian and the critic form the most useful part of the volume. The titles of some of these texts— "Dangers from Superficial Learning," "A Letter About Surrealism," "A Letter About Contemporary Art," "Poetic Understanding," "Contemporary Poetic and Artistic Problems"—reflect their content as well as their centrality in the evolution of twentieth-century Greek poetry and art. Elytis speaks with confidence not only because he is both a product of and a contributor to some of the topics he discusses, but also because of his familiarity with the work and thought of outstanding Greek and European figures who in some way or other left their mark on him, as revealed in his letters to them or in the essays devoted to them. The wide-ranging list includes such luminaries as Kálvos Theotokás, Embirícos, Gátsos, Papanoútsos, Theófilos (Elytis's monograph on Theófilos is included in its entirety in the "Open Book"), N. Hadjikyriákos-Ghíkas, Tsaroúhis, Móralis, Kaprálos, Phasianós, Picasso, John Veltri, Rimbaud, Lautréamont, Breton, Éluard, Pierre Jean Jouve, Federico García Lorca and Giuseppe Ungaretti.

It is important to remind ourselves that Elytis belongs to that fertile generation of the thirties which around the journal *Nea Ghrámmata* effected a revolution in Greek poetry and art. He tells the story of this "cultural revolution" in a large, fascinating and informative section entitled "The Chronicle of a Decade." The chronicle is a veritable serendipity of names and attitudes; and even though Elytis used it as an opportunity to develop in great detail his ideas on poetry, especially surrealism (culminating in the maxim that poetry is the other face of pride), he perhaps unknowingly made a lasting contribution to the cultural history of modern Greek. In my opinion, "The Chronicle of a Decade" should be translated into English as soon as possible, for it could serve as an excellent companion volume to the growing scholarship on Elytis in the English language. It contains some of the most powerful and most demanding passages in the entire volume, some of which could easily compare in expression and imagery with his finest verses. Considered along with his "texts," these passages amount to what could be described as Elytis's manifestoes on youth, love, Greece, poetry, art and life.

The "Open Book" is many books in one. Indeed, as mentioned above, the discussion on Theófilos had already been published separately, and "The Chronicle of a Decade" will most likely be published as an independent volume in the near future. All these books are held together admirably by the author's narrative skill and determination to challenge his native language to perform at the highest level possible. The result, although pleasant and undoubtedly rewarding, is at times extraordinarily demanding, as Elytis's labyrinthine thoughts occasionally require equally labyrinthine syntax from which one can extract the innermost meanings only with arduous efforts. For this and other reasons, such a brief description of the "Open Book" does the work an injustice. It merits careful study and analysis. The passages presented in the opening section of this issue, selected in consultation with the author, are intended as a small contribution in that direction.

The Imagery and Collages of Odysseus Elytis

By KIMON FRIAR

Just as Cavafis felt that, given other circumstances, he might have developed into a fine historian, so Elytis has felt that, had he been taught the rudiments of drawing at an early age, he might have developed into a fine painter. He does not regret, of course, that having had no other means, he turned to poetry. Indeed, he came to see that poetry, in its imagery, tones and compositional structure, contained elements of painting and architecture; in its phonetic orchestration and arrangements, the instrumentation and the forms of music; in dialogue, narrative or montage, techniques from the other arts.

Elytis's imagination always was—and continues to be—primarily an imagistic one. From the very first verses he wrote ("time is a swift shadow of birds / my eyes wide open within its images") to an as yet unpublished verse recently written ("one must transform every moment into an image") he finds that he has been impelled to apprehend mental, emotional and physical phenomena in no other way but through visualization and imagery. This is what gives his poetry its pictorial quality, its concreteness, its lack of generalization.

Nonetheless, a strong abstract element, even in his earlier verses, finds an outlet in the extraordinarily complicated, almost mathematically composed structures he has invented for many of his later poems, in "The Monogram," "The Light Tree and the Fourteenth Beauty," "The Stepchildren," and particularly in *The Axion Esti*, one of the most complicatedly constructed poems in modern times. "Image!" he exclaims, "O unvarying / outpouring of light / you enclose each hovering meaning / that allures our hope / toward composure"—and, it might be added, toward composition. Yet abstract design, proportion, synthesis are only the skeletal outlines of his poetic anatomy, fleshed out, given color, identification and analogy by a select and strange imagery of dreamlike invocation, supported, extended and given an esthetic base in early adolescence by his discovery of and dedication to surrealism.

At the age of eighteen, in 1929, he chanced upon a book of poems by Paul Éluard. In 1935, he heard a lecture on surrealism by Andréas Embirícos, who in that same year was to publish the first book of "automatic writing" poems in Greece, "Blast Furnace." In Embirícos's house the young man also saw for the first time original paintings by Max Ernst, Yves Tanguy and Oscar Dominquez. He discovered the fascination of collage and threw himself passionately into the creation of such puzzles, pasting together cutouts from various periodicals, letters of different colored inks, with strings, pebbles, wood. His first creations were the purely orthodox ones of paradoxical juxtapositions in imitation of the collages of Max Ernst, who, from engravings out of old books, put together strange and fantastic enigmas, much as in Lautréamont's revolutionary image, "as beautiful as the chance encounter on a dissecting table of a sewing machine and an umbrella." A few of these he exhibited at the First International Surrealist Exhibition in Athens (1935): amputated hands hanging from branches of trees, women with the heads of birds or horses.

Yet even at this period the young inventor realized that, though fascinated by these chance and curious propinquities, he must later give them more formal organization and yoke their uninhibited flight to some central theme, some purification of meaning. After the publication in 1939 of "Orientations," in which he gathered together his surrealist experiments in poetry, he devoted himself exclusively to the evolution of his imagination in the imagery of poetry and not of painting. It was not until many years later, in 1966, that he felt the need once again to return to pictorial expression. This time he painted some thirty-odd gouaches, which in their freshness and translucency, their clear colors and purity, reflected the poems he had been writing about the apotheosis of youth amid a dazzlement of Aegean seascape. Among these are 1) "Athos": Red roofs in the foreground, a sea for background on which Byzantine saints are arranged in ceremonial order as on an iconostasis. Boats disproportionately large sail between them, for, as he wrote in "Anniversary," "keels pass by, splitting some new obstacle / with passion and conquest." 2) "The Baptism": A facsimile of a Byzantine icon, but the one baptized is a lovely and naked adolescent girl. 3) "Mnisareti": Divided into two unequal and vertical sections. In the left section is Mnisareti as we know her in the famous stele of the early fourth century B.C., and in the right section are boats that sail above roofs and terraces. 4) "The Sorceress of Trees": A whitewashed wall implanted in the sea; to the left schematized shrubs and trees of various sizes; to the right a seated woman who holds a flame in her open palm, much as Elytis's mother, as he relates in his collection of prose writings, "Open Book," "kept vigil all night long, holding a fragment of moon in her hands." The image reflects that contained in an early poem, "Dionysos"—"scintillating in the palms of women who have embellished translucency"—and looks forward to another in *The Axion Esti*: "the stone hand of noon holding the sun in its open palm." These gouaches purified the absurdly contradictory images of his early collages into fanciful reconstructions characteristic also of his imagistic development as a poet.

A year later, in April, the colonels were to stomp over Greece with their tanks, their tortures and their censorship in an attempt to choke off all vital and therefore dangerous creative expression. The chance compilation in his flat of piles of periodicals with colored illustrations, a reluctance to publish and an inability to think or to create the more difficult imagery of poetry during a time of tyranny made Elytis turn once again to collage as a way out of his impasse. During the seven years from 1967 to the fall of the dictatorship in 1974, he created a series of about forty works, most of them in color and a few in black and white. Among those which I have had at my disposal are the nine published in his book of songs *Ta ro tou érota* (The Ro of Eros; Athens, Asterías, 1972), the nineteen in Ilías Petrópoulos's book *Elýtis, Móralis, Tsaroúhis* (Salonika, 1966) and many unpublished works shown me by the poet.

During his direct experimentations with painting in his gouaches, Elytis came to realize that it had become too late for him to attain to anything which might satisfy him technically as a painter. At the same time, he found that by setting aside the extravagances and curious juxtapositions of his earlier work, by concerning himself with purely plastic and compositional problems of color, synthesis, design, line, space, mass and proportion, and by utilizing the basic imagery of his poetry—seas, skies, shells, pebbles, waterdrops, stones, plants, flowers, fishes, birds, whitewashed island walls and homes, naked girls, ancient ruins and artifacts, Byzantine icons—he could, without treading on the claims of the painter, continue in another manner and in his own way the expressions of the same world which preoccupied him in his poetry and which corresponded to the same ideas. He found that he could now use the fully perfected images of painters and photographers and rearrange them to parallel the imagery of his poetry. He struggled within certain confines, for he had to work with whatever material was at hand, sometimes putting together these ready-made objects in ways to conform to a preconceived idea, but more often than not being directed by them, much as a sculptor may be directed by the quality, grain or size of a block of marble or of wood. Except for some occasional frustrations (he could not realize all he imagined or create works of large size), he found, as in his poetry, that such restrictions more often freed than hampered his imagination. Also, the element of chance, the necessity of creating out of the arbitrary and the ephemeral, had always fascinated him as one of the basic tenets of surrealism.

Although no clear division is possible, or even desirable, Elytis's collages may roughly be divided into two groups: 1) those that are somewhat abstract and modern, and 2) those that are poetically and Hellenically centered. Characteristic of both groups are an opposition to the contorted and the entangled and a tendency toward the Greek and the composed. In the more "abstract" collages he approaches his materials much as a painter sets out to solve problems of composition and synthesis. Colors and form must be placed just so and in no other way. A curve must find its analogy in some other curve, space must be balanced by space, mass by mass; line must be related to line, whether horizontally, vertically or obliquely; a bit of red must be adjusted with another red or a color of equal weight or intensity. As in cubism, as in architecture, as in poetry itself, one image, one mass must structurally be related to another. "Theme," if there is a theme at all, plays a minor role as such and is subordinated to the pure pleasures of esthetic canons.

In "Embroidery and Bird," for instance, (1974; *Elýtis, Móralis, Tsaroúhis*, p. 99), he cut out from a book of fabrics a rectangular sheet of light gray paper along whose bottom border was printed a horizontal wide band of woven crimson cloth with a geometric design in black, the handicraft of some Greek island, and from whose left edge hangs a wide tassel that not only breaks the symmetry of the design but also overlaps a narrower band of the same cloth without design a bit below and almost sheer with the end of the paper. Over this Elytis pasted, from a French book, the hollowed-out cross-section of an oval semiprecious stone whose inner outline suggests the shape of an embryo bird within an egg. The effect is that of an abstract composition with a hint of the representational.

In "Red Composition with Bicycle" (1974; ibid., p. 111), Elytis started out with a stylized outline drawing of the front section of a bicycle tied firmly with lock and chain to a pole, both against a yellow background. This he placed in the upper right of a dull, mottled red cutout, and this again on a vivid red sheet of paper broken along its length by a white vertical line placed almost at the far left. Below the bicycle he placed a black-green rectangle, interrupted in its lower left-hand corner by an elongated section of a brick wall, against which is silhouetted in black the head of a child. Black is continued obliquely and below to the left by what seems to be a section of a window or skylight opening into a dark night. At the bottom of the composition, an elongated black strip that slants up at the far right and then breaks into fragments completes and balances the dark tones. Stretched across the top of the bicycle and continued vertically down and below its left side in a wider swath is part of a gray-green wall with open windows revealing an azure sky with a hint of clouds. The effect is purely that of colors and proportions esthetically arranged, with the suggestion of a theme that relates the child's head with the bicycle and the fettered wheel with the open windows of freedom and escape, for nothing is *completely* abstract in any of Elytis's compositions. He is content, as in his poetry, to indulge his play with esthetics in the overall structure of his collages or poems that always contain some human or natural element.

In several instances Elytis has taken the well-known abstract paintings of Rothko as expressions of the modern spirit and imposed on them ancient archetypes, so as to place both in a timeless relationship, rendering them simultaneous and giving them another dimension through this conjoining. In "Delos" (1967; ibid., p. 106) he has placed the head and neck of one of the immediately recognizable lions of Delos in the upper of two blue-green rectangles followed by a third of mottled white, all set against an intense blue background. The two hues slightly suggest the colors of Greece, the mottled white the breaking foam of the sea. In "Idol" (1974, black-and-white; ibid., p. 109) he has adjusted an equally well-known Cycladic figure (c. 2000 B.C.) against a Rothko abstraction and further emphasized the amalgamation of times by bordering this along both sides with columnar cutouts taken from a scientific journal of modern abstract machines. In setting himself the problems of harmoniously wedding the archaic with the modern, time present with time past, he has unwittingly illustrated Eliot's proposition in "Burnt Norton" that "If all time is eternally present / All time is irredeemable. / What might have been is an abstraction" that remains "a perpetual possibility." This "perpetual possibility" is what has always fascinated Elytis's imagination. This same sense of condensed time has also impelled Elytis to use symbol or simile sparingly in his poems, for to him one object does not *represent* another nor is it *like* another. Rather, in an instantaneous identification, one object *is* the other, as in dream. So, in his collages, his girls are not symbols but simply *are*. When he places various cutouts side by side, they do not assume a metaphoric relationship but become fused into one another and exist monolithically in a newly created identity.

A similar sense of abstract design governs the collages that most imagistically correspond to Elytis's poetry of the Aegean. In "Aegean" (1974; ibid., p. 115) cutouts of whitewashed church domes from Santorini set against the sea, portions of whitewashed islandic walls, fragments of dappled green and gold sections taken from unrepresentational segments of Mycenaean death masks are all carefully balanced on an intense blue background. On the lower right of the rectangular depiction, hip and arm protruding slightly and thus breaking the vertical line, Elytis has tried, successfully, to combine a summery girl in rose (taken from Matisse) with photographic cutouts. To carry her color into the sky, he cut out the outline of a flying bird from a similar rose-colored paper and placed it in the air above the sea. Such birds abound in Elytis's poems as "infants of the wind" that "go to the morning inaugurations of the sea," that "nullify on high the weights of our hearts / and so much blue we have loved," whose song "hovers in mid-air / sowing the golden barley of fire / to the five winds / setting free a terrestrial beauty." In this collage, as in his poem "Event in August," "the girl's bird took a crumb of the sea and ascended."

In another collage, "Votive Offering" (1973; reproduced in this issue, p. 626), the whitewashed cubical houses of Skyros are viewed from the mountain on whose slope the village lies, so that their flat gray roofs form a jigsaw pattern of rectangles. In Elytis's creation, however, the mountain has vanished, and in its stead above the roofs extends a deep blue sea with a bare rugged island and a flat blue sky. To the left, emerging above the roofs from the waist up against sea, rock and sky, a Byzantine angel extends a hand as in a votive offering, which may be the triangular cluster of seashells turned inside-out, resembling a group of white angel trumpets announcing one of the Aegean's mysteries. Together with a few open-mouthed, reddish flowers, these cascade down from the roofs into another added sea, so that the town floats like a white island in an aqueous element. In one of his poems Elytis writes of "two seas again on either side," and of a "channel high above / changing the sky's ozone," for Greece is almost completely encircled by the sea. It is as if Elytis had depicted for us a variant of that lovely demotic distich: "Amid the blue Aegean waters come angels fluttering / And from the pulsing of their wings fall roses scattering." Two colorful strips from folk embroidery frame the collage at top and bottom, and above it rises the intricately carved woodwork of a Byzantine crown, from whose medallion Christ blesses a seascape which the poet and not His Father had created.

But perhaps the most enchanting and representative of all these collages is "Hovering Landscape with Angel" (1975, unpublished), which depicts Lasithi, that inland green valley of innumerable windmills in Crete, beloved by Elytis as the island of his birth and which he had always wished had been implanted by the sea. Rectifying an error made by nature, he has wedged onto this inland landscape a harbor filled with multicolored boats anchored on its created shores, and below the sea he has placed an inverted mountain and a sky again, so that both landscape and seascape float suspended in air. Indeed, in his poems, mulberry trees set sail on the grass's foam, the sun plants gardens on the surf, gardens enter the sea like promontories or bridal beds, and a cereal sea sustains huge cowsheds. Sea, sky and land in Greece are One. In the sky above the windmills is a young, angelic, full-breasted girl encased in a rosy seashell (heavenly Aphrodite born not out of the sea but out of the sky) whose wings are made of other seashells turned inside out to reveal their gloss of mother-of-pearl. She comes flying, bringing a message, her hand raised in benediction.

Somewhat similar is the "Angel of Astypalea" (1967; "The Ro of Eros," p. 12). where the hilltopped town of that Aegean island has been turned upside-down and wedged with its sky against whitewashed island houses, while a Byzantine angel floats against the landscape between the two skies. An island church floats across the top sky, balanced by a strip of bluish land that cuts across the bottom sky.

This brings us to the main motif of Elytis's collages: the apotheosis of naked young girls, of Eros and of girl-angels bringing mysterious and mystic messages, annunciations and benedictions, for they are the "Vessels of the Mysteries." "Angel," the poet exclaims in the poem *Villa Natacha*, "hover in flight around me somewhere . . . take me by the hand." This Angel with her "lean boyish body" is Arete in

"Sleep of the Valiant," both Greece and the Virgin Mary, all goodness, moral virtue, valor, glory, excellence of every kind, who descends to the Vast Dark Places of the world and labors to turn darkness into light.

In "The Fruit" (1974; *Elýtis, Móralis, Tsaroúhis*, p. 97) the face of a handsome dreaming girl has been substituted for that of the Virgin Mary in a holy icon. Before her have been placed, not church offerings of candles or incense, but nature's offerings of fruits, although flowers, shells or pebbles would have been equally appropriate for Elytis, as are the "leaves, fruits, flowers, many-branched dreams" he lists in "Pellucid Skies." As in his poems, this is "the girl who has not yet entered into love / but holds in her apron an acrid orchard of fruit" or gives "to the ritual of difficult dream a sure restoration." Her face, the "innocence we had found so enigmatic," is "washed by a dawn we loved because we did not know that within us, even deeper still, we were preparing other larger dreams that must hug in their arms more earth, more blood, more water, more fire, more Love." "In the arms of the Virgin," Elytis writes in "Open Book," "I placed flowers, and in the arms of Saints, girls and birds."

In "Girl on a Calyx" (1974; ibid., p. 98), reclining on a huge red calyx growing out of luxurious green leaves on a black background, a girl is sleeping naked in the sun. She is "the blond and sunburnt girl" we meet in Elytis's poems sleeping in "the azure light on the stone steps of August," the one who is "intoxicated with the sun's juices," the "sunburnt and scintillating girl—lullaby of eyelids on the mythical spaciousness of the world." Elytis's collages are not literal depictions of his poems but simply utilize similar images, adapted as his materials direct. At times, indeed, he may take over into his poetry an image he has first created in a collage, as in a recent unpublished poem using this image of a sleeping girl sunning herself on the calyx of a red flower. There has always been an interchange flowing from his poems to his collages; now an opposite flow is beginning, thus establishing a genuine interrelationship.

"The Railing" (1975; ibid., p. 105) depicts a bare-breasted woman enclosed in railings cut out of mottled paper in various lights and shades. Her flimsy flowery shawl reveals a hint of "that bit of black in the nook" of the thighs, a "glimpse of the sea-urchin / for a moment / in sea-depths unexplored." On her right, from top to bottom, falls a cascade of large leaves, from highly polished, glossy green to dappled shades of rose and yellow. She is indeed that "patrician lady of grasses," that green girl of whom the poet says "I shall enter from the door that a plain leaf protects." Although the leaves are not those of a "celestial eucalyptus," they too are bitten by the poet, so that "the holy day of sensual pleasure may emit its fragrance." But most inspiringly, this is the woman whom the bearded man in "On the Republic" frees from her cage, who then turns into a bird that hovers motionless above the peristyle of the poet's Temple and becomes a naked woman again "with a green mist on her hair and a jacket of golden wire," sitting on the tiles "with her thighs half open." And this, says the poet, "in my consciousness took on the meaning of a flower when danger opens within it its first tenderness." He receives this celestial vision as in a wet dream, and then continues to write frenziedly "among large transparent leaves" to sanction and bless all forms of lovemaking in his Republic of poetry and collage, as diversified as "the various ways birds have of flying little by little / as far as the infinite." "When you glitter in the sun that on you glides water-drops, and deathless hyacinths, and silences," the poet exclaims in "The Concert of Hyacinths," "I proclaim you the only reality."

One is almost convinced, both in Elytis's poems and in his collages, that the beautiful, naked body of a young girl, a distillation of sunlight and dewdrops, is indeed the only reality; that in its purity and innocence it arouses sexual desire to the highest pitch of holiness. A girl-angel in flight bringing benediction is surely, and not only in Freudian terms, an intense if unconscious symbol of erotic sanctity. "A naked body," he writes in a yet unpublished poem, "is the only extension of that immaterial line that unites us with the Mystery." These are his "grapehard girls," "seablue to the bone," who "run naked in men's eyes" while "innocence / strips itself of its last lie." These "naked bodies carved on the pediments of time" are Ersi, Mirto, Roxani, Fotini, Anna, Alexandra, Cynthia, whom he invokes and glorifies in the last section of *The Axion Esti*, "Marina as she was before she existed." For Elytis, whatever is natural is holy, and the five or more senses are sacred portals to an earthly as well as to a celestial paradise. "I have never as yet found sorrow in the flesh," he writes in "Open Book," contradicting Mallarmé. For a love to be truly love, it must be "true and free, above and beyond the rumpled bedsheets of religion and country."

In "The Small Rose" (1967; ibid., p. 100) a naked girl wearing a necklace of leaves and what may be a semiprecious stone or seashell resembling a large drop of water and crowned with a huge rose, rises out of rock and sea and extends into a classic Doric temple. In "Nude" (1974; ibid., p. 104) a naked girl with head bowed and hands hanging limply before her in the posture of reverence in church is placed against the backdrop of a huge angel's hand from some Byzantine icon in the ceremonious gesture of benediction. In the collage which is deceptively and yet appropriately entitled "Portrait" (1968; ibid., p. 114) we are pleasingly startled to find in a golden Byzantine icon the clear-eyed face of a lovely girl with flowing blond hair gazing at us from where the face of Christ should have been, thus identifying male and female in that pristine stage of their early origins as related by Diotima in Plato's *Symposium*. In "The Two Friends" (1974; ibid., p. 112) two naked girls are placed side by side, their loving and joyous glances interwined, while around their hands float orbs of mosaic stone and erect, slender, dark leaves rise like phalli. Encircling their heads, as in a single halo, is the gold-framed painting of a Renaissance angel kneeling before the lilies of annunciation. These girls, like the one in "The Small Rose," wear between their breasts what may be a semiprecious stone but which, in effect, for Elytis, is a large luminous drop of water, the "clover of light" which Marina of the Rocks wears in his poem by that name. In "Open Book" he writes of "naked girls flying and unwinding blond manes made of thousands of glittering water-drops." The various orbs which at times surround his girls or angels and which they often carry also resemble floating drops of water that have captured the essence of light.

In "Open Book" Elytis recalls how his island nurses exorcised the Evil Eye by babbling incoherent words while holding in their hands the small leaf of some humble plant. "This small leaf with the unknown powers of innocence," he writes, "and the strange words that accompany it, is Poetry herself." In his travels throughout Greece he ascertained that its landscapes and seascapes were laden with secret messages expressed in what seemed to be incoherent sounds, yet heavy with "the meaning and weight of a secret and mystic mission." Voices "arrived from the unknown, half questions and half tyrannical oracles, meteors of the middle distance, fragments of consciousness that glide on the lips of Sirens and which the wind reaped." In his dreams he heard leaves speaking, one by one. When he gazed mesmerized on a lizard palpitating in a shaft of sun on a rock, or on dolphins in starlight stitching a ceaseless embroidery in and out of the sea, or on a butterfly alighting on the heaving breast of a young girl sleeping in the sun, it was as if an archangel, in the form of a beautiful young girl, had come to bring, not an annunciation for the Virgin only, but messages from nature as well, in sounds which, if rightly deciphered, would reveal the mystery of this life, of "this small, this great world."

It is, of course, the nature of these revelations to be forgotten the moment they are instinctively decoded. The only thing the poet can do is to try to catch their revelations in the half-notation that is poetry, to catch "a metaphysic wherein the phenomenon of language is a musical notation of many meanings . . . an ethical power which the human mind invokes, in exactly the same manner in which a landscape is not at all the rustling of a few trees." Many of the poems in "The Light Tree and the Fourteenth Beauty" deal with this theme. In "Three Times the Truth" we read: "The wild bird *pit-pit* shifted truth from one rock to another / . . . Something must *assuredly* exist / . . . And everywhere out of springs and rosemary an *Our Father* rose like a confession / . . . Something dæmonic but which can be caught in the shape of an Archangel as in a net / . . . I didn't hear / what did you say? / —*Adýss, adýss, adíze* / Until . . . I felt . . . that out of nothing is born our Paradise." And in "The Odyssey" we find: "A girl suddenly / struck by an Archangel's glance / whom I took as my slave / and even today as I write only she has stood by me." But it is particularly in "The Girl the North Wind Brought" that the girl-angel appears in annunciation to the poet: "up there . . . gaining in height / and as beautiful as can be / with all the whimsies of birds in her movements . . . / leaning her small breasts for the wind to withstand." In startled revelation, the poet testifies: "a terrified joy within me mounted to my eyelids and fluttered there / . . . / Kindred orbs of light burst behind her and left in the sky / something like the elusive signs of Paradise."

In "Sophia Erect" (1974; ibid., p. 101) an archangel with the face of a girl is holding in her left hand an "orb of light" much like a radiating star, while below and around her float other orbs—stars, planets or dewdrops. The girls in "The Two Friends" have such orbs at their sides. In "Inverted Landscape" (1968; "The Ro of Eros," p. 68) an angel comes bearing such an orb, while others fall like huge drops of water from one sky to another. "Nude," "Portrait," "The Angel of Astypalea" and "Hovering Landscape with Angel" all realize in collage Elytis's apotheosis of girls receiving or bestowing benediction and bringing revelations of nature's divinity.

It remains only to note that the most prominent image by far in Elytis's poetry—the Sovereign Sun, incarnation of all metaphysical and ethical light, of all Justice—is nowhere to be found in any of his collages. It may be that this poet, this "sun-drinker" who has rarely seen a sunrise, who writes best far into the night, for whom the sun's "divine vertical," in Alexander Mátsas's phrase, is not shaken "in the purification of absolute noon," finds the sun too banal as a photographed or painted image, where it is deprived of its metaphysical extensions. And though he has equally hymned the adolescent Aegean lad, the "patriot of the sun," the "gamin of the white cloud," the "child with skinned knee," the "sailor boy of the garden" and the young Second Lieutenant of the Albanian campaign who "ascends alone and blazing with light," only one very lovely collage, "Small Eros" (1967; ibid., p. 57), depicts a small boy with trefoil wings rimmed with large drops of water as he treads the air over a mountain slope that descends in terraces from powdered blue to powdered green. Perhaps all the boys, all the young men in his poems, are the poet himself, narcissistically one, while his girls are all women everywhere, all revelation, all angels announcing the holy wedding of the flesh and the spirit.

Chronology

1911	2 November: Born Odysseás Alepoudhélis in Iráklion, Crete, of parents from Lesbos.
1914	Family moves to Athens.
1917–1923	Attends the Makrís Grade School.
1923–1928	Attends the Third Gymnasium.
1929	Reads a book of poems by Paul Éluard, first contact with surrealism.
1930–1935	Attends the School of Law, University of Athens, but leaves without taking his degree.
1935	Hears Andréas Embiríkos lecture on surrealism. Experiments with automatic writing and fantastic collages. Exhibits collages in First International Surrealist Exhibition in Athens. Publishes a group, "First Poems," in periodical, *Nea Ghrámata* (New Letters), Athens.
1936	Publishes group of poems, "Orientations," in periodical, *Makedhonikés Iméres* (Macedonian Days).
1937	Publishes poem, "Hourglass of the Unknown," in "Macedonian Days."
1939	Publishes group of poems, "In the Service of Summer," in "Macedonian Days." December: Publishes book, "Orientations" (Athens, Pirsós, 180 pp.)
1940–1941	Serves as Second Lieutenant in First Army Corps on Albanian Front.
1943	December: Publishes book, "Sun the First together with Variations on a Sunbeam" (Athens, O Gláros [The Gull], 44 pp.).
1945	Publishes "Heroic and Elegiac Song for the Lost Second Lieutenant of the Albanian Campaign," in periodical, *Tetrádhio* (Notebook), No. 2, pp. 9–13.
1945–1946	Director of Programming and Broadcasting for the National Broadcasting Institute, Athens.
1946	Publishes poem, "Kindness in the Wolfpasses," in *Tetrádhio*, pp. 3–14.
1948	Regular literary critic for the newspaper, *Kathimerini* (Daily). Represents Greece in the Second International Gathering of Modern Painters, Geneva. Begins writing *The Axion Esti*.
1948–1952	Settles in Paris, studying literature at the Sorbonne. Travels in England, Switzerland, Italy, Spain. Associates with Breton, Éluard, Tzara, Char, Jouve, Michaux, Ungaretti, Matisse, Picasso, Giacometti, de Chirico. Collaborates with the periodical, *Verve*.
1950	Participates in the First International Conference of Art Critics, Paris. Elected member of The International Union of Art Critics.
1953	Returns to Greece. Elected member of the poetry committee of The Group of Twelve which annually gave awards in poetry, drama and essay writing.
1953–1954	Director of Programming and Broadcasting for the National Broadcasting Institute, Athens.
1954	Is elected a member of the Société Européenne de Culture in Venice.
1955–1956	On the Governing Board of Károlos Koún's Art Theatre.
1956–1958	President of the Governing Board of the Greek Ballet.
1959	Publishes book of poems, *To Áxion Estí* (Athens, Íkaros, 94 pp.).

1960	Publishes book of poems, "Six and One Remorses for the Sky" (Athens, Íkaros, 30 pp.). Awarded the National Prize in Poetry for *To Áxion Estí*.
1961	March through June: tours the United States at the invitation of the Department of State. Paperback reprint of "Orientations" (Athens, Galaxy).
1962	December: At the invitation of the Soviet Union, visits Odessa, Moscow, Leningrad. Publishes in book form "Heroic and Elegiac Song for the Lost Second Lieutenant of the Albanian Campaign" (Athens, Íkaros, 40 pp.). 25 December: Publishes "Albaniad. Poems for Two Voices. First Part" in periodical, *Panspoudhastikí*, No. 41, pp. 11–14.
1964	*The Axion Esti* set to music by Míkis Theodhorákis.
1965–1968	Member of the Administrative Board of the Greek National Theatre. Is awarded the Order of the Phoenix.
1966	Paints some 30-odd gouaches; destroys all but four.
1967–1974	Creates a series of about forty collages.
1969–1971	Lives in France, primarily in Paris.
1970	Spends summer in Cyprus.
1971	Publishes poem, "Death and Resurrection of Konstandínos Paleológhos," in periodical, *Tram*, Salonika, pp. 30–32. Publishes "Death and Resurrection of Konstandínos Paleológhos" in book form (Geneva, Duo d'Art, 16 pp.); silk-screen handwritten text and four embossed designs by Cóstas Colentianós; one hundred eleven copies, numbered and signed by the artist and the poet. Publishes poem, "The Monogram" (Famagústa, Cyprus, L'Oiseau, 32 pp.; printed in the poet's handwriting by Joseph Adam, Brussels). December: Publishes poems, "The Sovereign Sun" (Athens, Íkaros, 32 pp.). Publishes book of poems, "The Light Tree and the Fourteenth Beauty" (Athens, Íkaros, 70 pp.).
1972	November: Publishes book of songs, "The Ro of Eros," with nine collages, eight in color and one in black-and-white. (Athens, Asterías, 98 pp.). December: Publishes poem, "The Monogram," as a regular book (Athens, Íkaros, 32 pp.).
1973	June: Publishes poem, *Villa Natacha* (Salonika, Tram, 20 pp.) with an original sketch by Picasso, a colored lithograph by Laurens and decorations by Matisse from the periodical, *Verve*. December: Publishes poem, "The Leaf Diviner," broadsheet (Athens, Asterías, 2 pp.). Publishes book of art criticism, "The Painter Theófilos" (Athens, Asterías).
1974	September: Publishes collected essays, "Open Book" (Athens, Asterías, 520 pp.). December: Publishes book of poems, "The Stepchildren" (Athens, Íkaros, 64 pp.). Publishes nineteen collages, ten in color and nine in black-and-white in Ilías Petrópoulos's book *Elýtis, Móralis, Tsaroúhis* (Athens, Pleías, 164 pp.). *The Sovereign Sun* (Philadelphia, Temple University Press, 200 pp.), largest selection of his poems in English, translated by Kimon Friar. *The Axion Esti* (Pittsburgh, University of Pittsburgh Press, 159 pp.), bilingual edition, translated by Edmund Keeley and George Savidis.

1975   Visits France in Spring. Autumn issue of *Books Abroad* dedicated to him. Becomes Honorary Citizen of Mytilene. Receives Honorary Doctorate from the University of Salonika.

1976   Publishes collected poetry translations, "Second Writing" (Athens, Ikaros, 211 pp.). *The Axion Esti* is performed in the Odeon of Herod Atticus in Athens and in the Lycabettus Theatre, with Mikis Theodorakis conducting the orchestra in his own composition.

1977   The National Theatre in Athens presents "The Great Hour," a series of performances of compositions inspired by Elytis's verse.

1978   The Greek journal *Aiólika Ghrámata* (Aeolian Letters) dedicates its January-April issue (numbers 43–44) to Elytis (191 pp.). Publishes *María Neféli*.

1979   Publishes 220-page anthology of selected writings 1935–77, *Ekloyí*, which contains, besides poems, excerpts from his essays, eight collages in color, selected essays on his work by other critics (1938–77) and a basic bibliography. Translations of this representative selection are scheduled to appear in Polish, Romanian and other languages. As the second Greek after George Seferis (1963), Elytis wins the Nobel Prize for Literature: "For his poetry, which, against the background of Greek tradition, depicts with sensuous strength and intellectual clearsightedness modern man's struggle for freedom and creativeness."

1980   Awarded honorary doctorate from Sorbonne University. "Elytis Nights" in Bonn, Brussels and other European capitals. *Odysseus Elytis: Analogies of Light*, an updated and enlarged version of the Autumn 1975 Elytis issue of *Books Abroad*, is published in book form by the University of Oklahoma Press.

Selected Bibliography (1939-1979)

POETRY

1939   *Prosanatolizmí* (Orientations), Athens, Pirsós. Republished in 1961, Athens, Galaxy.

1943   *Ílios o prótos, mazí me tis parallayiés páno se mián ahtídha* (Sun the First together with Variations on a Sunbeam), Athens, O Gláros.

1945   *Ázma iroikó ke pénthimo yia ton haméno anthipolohaghó tis Alvanías* (Heroic and Elegiac Song of the Lost Second Lieutenant of the Albanian Campaign), *Tetrádhio* [Notebook], no. 2, August–September, pp. 9–13. Republished in 1962, Athens, Íkaros.

1946   "I kalosíni stis likoporiés" (Kindness in the Wolfpasses), *Tetrádhio*, December, pp. 3–14.

1959   *To Áxion Estí*, Athens, Íkaros.

1960   *Éxi ke miá típsis yia ton uranó* (Six and One Remorses for the Sky), Athens, Íkaros.

1962   "Alvaniádha. Píima yia dhió phonés. Méros próto" (Albaniad. Poems for Two Voices. First Part), *Panspoudhastikí*, no. 41, 25 December, pp. 11–14.

1971   *O ílios o iliátoras* (The Sovereign Sun), Athens, Íkaros. *Thánatos ke Anástasis tou Konstandínou Paleológhou* (Death and Resurrection of Constandínos Paleológhos), *Tram* [Salonika], December, pp. 30–32. Republished as silk-screen handwritten text in 1971. Geneva, Duo d'Art. *To Monóghrama* (The Monogram), Famagústa, Cyprus, L'Oiseau. Republished in 1972, Athens, Íkaros. *To fotódhendro ke i dhekáti tetárti omorfiá* (The Light Tree and the Fourteenth Beauty), Athens, Íkaros.

1972   *Ta ro tou érota* (The Ro of Eros), Athens, Asterías.

1973   *Villa Natacha*, Salonika, Tram, with an original sketch by Picasso, a colored lithograph by Laurens and decorations by Matisse from the periodical, *Verve*. *O fillomándis* (The Leaf Diviner; broadsheet), Athens, Asterías.

1974   *Ta eterothalí* (The Stepchildren), Athens, Íkaros.

1977   *Simatolóyion* (The Book of Signs), Athens, Ermías.

1978   *María Neféli* (Maria Cloud), Athens, Íkaros.

1979   *Ekloyí 1935–1977* (Selected Writings), Athens, Akmon.

PROSE AND OTHER WORKS

1973   *O zoghráfos Theófilos* (The Painter Theófilos), Athens, Asterías.

1974   *Anihtá hártia* (Open Book), Athens, Asterías.

1976   *Imayía tou Papadhiamándhi* (The Magic of Papadhiamándhis), Athens, Ermías. *Dhéfteri ghrafí* (Second Writing; translations of Rimbaud, Lautréamont, Éluard, Jouve, Ungaretti, García Lorca, Mayakovsky), Athens, Íkaros.

1978   *Anaforá ston Embiríko* (Reference to Embirikos; essay), Salonika, Egnatía.

TRANSLATIONS

1945 *Poèmes* [bilingual], Robert Levesque, tr., Athens, Asterías.

1952 *Odisseo Elitis: Poesie*, Mario Vitti, tr., Rome. "Poesie precedute del canto eroico e funebre per il sottotenente caduta in Albania," Mario Vitti, tr., *Il Presente* [Rome], June. *New World Writing No. 2*, Kimon Friar, tr., New York, New American Library. *Little Treasury of World Poetry*, Hugh Creekmore, ed., Kimon Friar, tr., New York, Scribner's.

1953 Kimon Friar, "The Greek Tradition" and translations of selected poems, *Wake 12* [Boston], Winter number.

1954 Kimon Friar, "Odysseus Elýtis" and translations of selected poems, plus two letters by Elytis, *Accent* [Urbana, Il.], Summer number.

1957 "Drinking the Sun of Corinth," "The Mad Pomegranate Tree," Edmund Keeley, tr., *The Beloit Poetry Journal*, Spring number. Edmund Keeley, translations of selected poems, *The Antioch Review*, Autumn number.

1959 Maria-Louise Arserin, *Anthologie des poètes néogrecs*, Rome.

1960 *Körper des Sommers* [selected poems], Antigone Kasoléa and Barbara Schlörb, trs., St. Gallen, Tschudy. *Six Poets of Modern Greece*, Edmund Keeley and Philip Sherrard, trs., London, Thames & Hudson; New York, Knopf, 1961. Otto Staininger, *Griechische Lyrik der Gegenwart*, Linz, J. Wimmer. Kimon Friar, translations of selected poems, plus "Odysseus Elytis: A Critical Mosiac" by Mítsos Papanikoláou, Andréas Karandónis, Samuel Baud-Bovy, Nános Valaorítis, Kimon Friar and Níkos Gâtsos, *The Charioteer* [New York], Autumn number. Two poems, Edmund Keeley, tr., *Western Humanities Review*, Winter number.

1962 "The Mad Pomegranate Tree," Edmund Keeley, tr., *The Guinness Book of Poetry 5*, London, Putnam.

1964 Edmund Keeley, "'The Genesis': A Commentary" and translations of selected poems, Edmund Keeley, Philip Sherrard and Ruth Whitman, trs., *Poetry* [Chicago], October.

1966 *Four Greek Poets*, Edmund Keeley and Philip Sherrard, trs., Harmondsworth, Penguin (same Elytis selections as in *Six Poets of Modern Greece*). Two poems in *The Penguin Book of Modern Verse Translation*, Keeley and Sherrard, trs., George Steiner, ed., Harmondsworth, Penguin. *Modern European Poetry*, Willis Barnstone, ed., Kimon Friar, tr. [Greek section], New York, Bantam. *Sieben nächtliche Siebenzeiler*, Günter Dietz, tr., Darmstadt, Bläschke.

1967 "The *Axion estí* of Odysseus Elytis" [dissertation], translated and annotated with an introduction by George Niketas, University of Georgia.

1968 *Elitis, 21 Poesie*, Vincenzo Rotolo, tr., Palermo, Instituto Siciliano di Studi Bizantini e Neoellenici.

1969 *Introduction to Modern Greek Literature*, Mary Gianos, ed., Kimon Friar, tr. [poetry selection], New York, Twayne. *To Áxion Estí—Gepriesen Sei*, Günter Dietz, tr., Hamburg, Claassen. "The Axion Esti, Part III," Edmund Keeley and George Savidis, trs., *Agenda*, Winter number.

1971   *Modern Greek Poetry*, 2nd rev. and enl. ed., Rae Dalven, tr., New York, Russell
       & Russell. *The Penguin Book of Greek Verse* [bilingual, with prose translations],
       Constantine A. Trypanis, ed., Harmondsworth, Penguin. Miguel Castillo, *Anto-
       logía de la literatura neohelénica. I: Poesía*, Santiago, Chile.

1973   Kimon Friar, *Modern Greek Poetry: From Caváfis to Elýtis*, New York, Simon
       & Schuster.

1974   *The Sovereign Sun: Selected Poems*, Kimon Friar, tr., Philadelphia, Temple Uni-
       versity Press. *The Axion Esti* [bilingual edition], Edmund Keeley and George
       Savidis, trs., Pittsburgh, University of Pittsburgh Press.

1977   *Six plus un remords pour le ciel*, F. B. Mâche, tr., Montpellier, Fata Morgana
       (2nd printing, 1979).

1979   *Axion Esti: Lovad Vare*, Ingemar Rhedin, tr. [Swedish], Stockholm, Bonniers.
       Sex och ett amvetskval för himlen, Lasse Söderberg, Mikael Fioretis, trs. [Swed-
       ish], Stockholm, FIB:s Lyrikklub / Tiden Förlag. *Ausgewählte Gedichte*, Barbara
       Vierneisel-Schlörb, Antigone Kasolea, trs. Frankfurt a.M., Suhrkamp (bilingual
       ed.). *To Áxion Estí—Gepriesen Sei*, Günter Dietz, tr., Hamburg, Claassen (2nd.
       ed.).

1980   *Maria Neféli*, Athan Anagnostopoulos, tr., New York, Houghton Mifflin (forth-
       coming).

VARIA

1946   Nános Valaorítis, "Modern Greek Poetry," *Horizon* [London], March.

1947   Robert Levesque, *Domaine Grec (1930–1946)*, Geneva, Trois Collines.

1962   Jaime García Terrés, *Grecia 60: Poesía y verdad*, Alacená,Mexico.

1971   Tásos Lighnádhis, *To Áxion Estí tou Elíti: Isaghoyí, Skholiazmós, Análisi*

1980   Andhréas Karandhónis, *Yia ton Odysséa Elýti* (About Odysseus Elytis; essays
       and reviews from the 1940s through *Maria Neféli*), Athens, Papadhímas.

ODYSSEUS ELYTIS IN
BOOKS ABROAD / WORLD LITERATURE TODAY
(1962–1980)

1. *Körper des Sommers*, Barbara Schlörb, tr. (St. Gallen, Tschudy, 1960), reviewed
   by Michael Rethis in *BA* 36:1, pp. 111–12.

2. Kimon Friar, "Odysseus Elýtis" in *BA* 45:2, pp. 225–30.

3. "3 Poems: Shape of Boeotia, Laconic, Psalm II," translated by Kimon Friar in
   BA 45:2, pp. 230–31.

4. Tásos Lighnádhis, *To Áxion Estí tou Elíti* (Athens, Vivliothíki Skholís Moraíti,
   1971), reviewed by Kimon Friar in *BA* 47:3, p. 598.

5. *To fotódhendro ke i dhékati tétarti omorfiá* (Athens, Íkaros, 1971), reviewed by
   Kimon Friar in *BA* 47:3, pp. 599–600.

6. *Thánatos ke Anástasi tou Konstandínou Paleológhou* (Geneva, Duo d'Art, 1971),
   reviewed by Kimon Friar in *BA* 47:3, pp. 599–600.

7. *Monóghrama* (Famagústa, L'Oiseau, 1971), reviewed by Kimon Friar in *BA* 47:4, pp. 809–10.

8. *Ta ro tou érota* (Athens, Asterías, 1972), reviewed by Kimon Friar in *BA* 48:1, p. 195.

9. *O ílios o iliátoras* (Athens, Íkaros, 1971), reviewed by Kimon Friar in *BA* 48:1, p. 195.

10. *Villa Natacha* (Salonika, Tram, 1973), reviewed by Kimon Friar in *BA* 48:3, p. 614.

11. *The Axion Esti*, Edmund Keeley and George Savidis, trs. (Pittsburgh, University of Pittsburgh Press, 1974), reviewed by Kimon Friar in *BA* 49:4, pp. 829–30.

12. *Ta eterothalí* (Athens, Íkaros, 1974), reviewed by Kimon Friar in *BA* 49:4, pp. 824–25.

13. *The Sovereign Sun*, Kimon Friar, tr. (Philadelphia, Temple University Press, 1974), reviewed by Andonis Decavalles in *BA* 49:4, pp. 830–31.

14. "Analogies of Light: The Greek Poet Odysseus Elytis," in *BA* 49:4, pp. 627–716.

15. Nikolaos Kálas, *Odhós Nikíta Rándou*, Odysseus Elytis, foreword (Athens, Ikaros, 1977), reviewed by Andonis Decavalles in *WLT* 52:4, pp. 673–74.

16. Mario Vitti, with Angelikís Ghavathá, *Odhysséas Elýtis: Vivlioghrafía 1935–1971* (Athens, Ikaros, 1977), reviewed by Andonis Decavalles in *WLT* 52:4, p. 647.

17. *I mayía tou Papadhiamándhi* (Athens, Ermías, 1978), reviewed by Andonis Decavalles in *WLT* 54:1, p. 149.

18. Ivar Ivask, "Greek Poet Odysseus Elytis, Nobel 1979, and Czech Novelist Josef Škvorecký, Neustadt 1980," in *WLT* 54:2, pp. 189–91.

19. M. Byron Raizis, "1979 Nobel Laureate Odysseus Elytis: From *The Axion Esti* to *María Neféli*" in *WLT* 54:2, pp. 196–201.